P9-DHT-552

D0014915

D0014913

BASEBALL'S HOMETOWN TEAMS

BASEBALL'S HOMETOWN TEAMS

THE STORY OF THE MINOR LEAGUES

BRUCE CHADWICK

ABBEVILLE PRESS   PUBLISHERS

NEW YORK   LONDON   PARIS

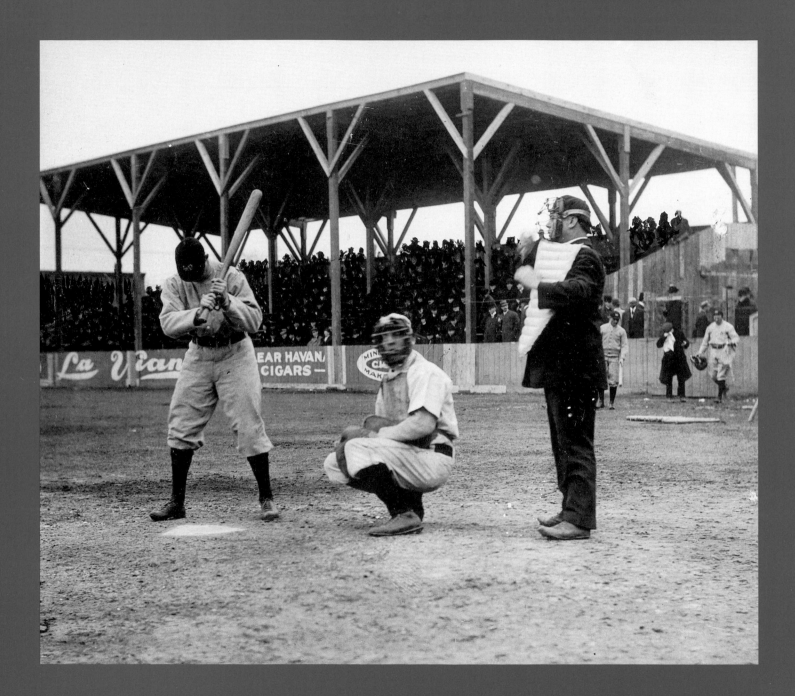

CONTENTS

COLLECTORS FROM ALL OVER THE WORLD BUY MEMORABILIA OF THE DURHAM BULLS, AN AMERICAN PHENOMENON AFTER THE 1988 FILM "BULL DURHAM."

INTRODUCTION

The man and his son were lost. They had missed the small side street that cuts between the mammoth old red-brick tobacco warehouses and leads to the Durham Athletic Park. The man kept peering out the rolled-down windows of the car looking for the ballpark and his son kept gently punching his baseball mitt with a clenched fist, getting ready for all the foul balls he was sure would come his way this warm July night. Suddenly, over the tops of the warehouses, the man heard John Fogerty's baseball song "Centerfield" wafting through the air. He stopped, turned around, and drove toward the music.

He drove through the warehouses and began to see people on their way to watch the Durham Bulls play ball. A battalion of young women from nearby Duke University, wearing gray school tee-shirts, waited on the long line to buy tickets (most cost three bucks) at the orange booth shaped like a castle turret with a huge bull jumping through a large "D" above the ticket window. Two old men wearing blue Durham Bulls jackets, their hands thrust deep in their pockets, had a heated discussion that jumped back and forth between baseball and politics. A woman calmly waited on the corner, a small child clutching each of her hands, a program tucked under her arm. Two teenagers played catch, arching the ball high above the cars driving between them.

Parents and their children walked down the city streets to the tiny, brightly painted, orange and blue ballpark, set down in a small hollow of land wedged between the warehouses where the people of Durham have worked in the tobacco industry for 150 years.

Inside the old ballpark, built in 1924 and rebuilt after a 1939 fire, ballplayers were unwinding by trotting across the outfield, which runs uphill. The starting pitcher threw a few hard ones to the catcher and you could hear the "pop" the ball makes when it hits the glove all over the ballpark. (The five thousand seats are so close to the infield that the dust from a slide into home plate settles in your lap.) Bullpen pitchers lazily threw balls to each other and talked to the kids leaning over the right-field fence. Ballplayers walking to the field stopped, as they always do, to sign dozens of autographs. Alice Cook, age seventy-four, in a new white dress ("makes me look thin"), took her seat. She has been going to Bulls games since the 1930s, when she met her husband at the ballpark. The woman who is the Carolina Chicken (a mascot who travels around the state on the baseball circuit) pulled on her enormous chicken head and prepared for work, complaining that Durham's mascot, Wool E. Bull, has an air-conditioning unit in his suit. The voice on the PA system thanked everyone for boards for local stores like the Well Spring Grocery and the Lone Star Steak House. All the seats under the tin roof are practically on top of the field. The players are young and enthusiastic, certain they'll soon be major-league stars.

The minors have been in business since 1877. Everyone knows that players drafted by major-league clubs are assigned to teams in the minors and move up through the ranks on their way to the big leagues. Some of them make it. Most don't. Now and then broadcasters who used to be ballplayers will tell a funny anecdote about the minors and

THESE RATHER CASUAL SLUGGERS, POSED IDENTICALLY, PLAYED FOR TORONTO ABOUT 1919.

coming and reminded one and all that on the following Sunday all tickets—and hot dogs—would be sold for just twenty-five cents. At a few minutes past 7:30 the Bulls ran on to the field for the game. The forty-foot-tall Durham Bull, which stands behind the right-field fence, roared, wagged its tail, blinked its electronic red eyes, and snorted smoke. The umpire yelled, "Play ball!" The crowd roared.

The lovely old Durham Athletic Park, made famous in the 1988 film *Bull Durham*, is a typical minor-league ball-park. The outfield walls are covered with advertising

THE GREAT LEFTY GROVE (LEFT) WON TWENTY GAMES EVERY YEAR BUT WAS HELD BACK IN THE MINORS BY OWNER DUNN FOR FOUR YEARS, UNTIL DUNN FINALLY GOT HIS PRICE ON THE PITCHER—$100,001 (THE EXTRA DOLLAR WAS TO TOP THE $100,000 THE RED SOX PAID FOR BABE RUTH).

JACK DUNN (CENTER), WITH MANAGER IN THE ORIOLES
DUGOUT, BOUGHT THE TEAM IN 1907 AND TURNED IT INTO
A MINOR-LEAGUE LEGEND.

I'VE ALWAYS LOVED MINOR-LEAGUE BALL.
MY DAD WAS A BIG FAN, AND HE TOOK ME
TO GAMES. NOW I BRING MY OWN KIDS. I HOPE
THEY'LL BRING THEIR KIDS.

—TRACEY DENNIS,
OF WYOMISSING, PENNSYLVANIA

THE DURHAM BULLS PLAYED ONE SEASON IN THE NORTH CAROLINA LEAGUE (1902) AND THEN RETURNED AS AN ENTRY IN THE NORTH CAROLINA STATE LEAGUE IN 1913, WHEN THIS PICTURE WAS TAKEN. THE ORIGINAL BULL DURHAM SIGN IS BEHIND THEM. THE BULLS LATER PLAYED IN THE PIEDMONT AND CAROLINA LEAGUES. THEY MOVED TO A BRAND-NEW BALLPARK IN 1994.

MR. WOOL E. BULL, THE DURHAM BULLS' MASCOT.

now and then major leaguers will grouse about being sent down to the minors for a week or two of rehabilitation. Everybody knows a little bit about baseball's second tier. This book tells the complete story of the minors and why baseball, its players, and its fans are wildly different there.

You don't see security agents breaking up fights at minor-league parks. You don't see drunks. You don't see ushers holding back kids looking for autographs from the ballplayers. Parking is almost always free. Tickets are rarely more than three dollars, and in many towns you can sit

SARANAC LAKE WAS A RESORT COMMUNITY IN UPSTATE NEW YORK. THIS SEMIPRO
TEAM PLAYED OTHERS IN THE AREA FOR THE AMUSEMENT OF VACATIONERS
IN THE LATE 1940S.

are as comfortable as a favorite chair. Beer costs a buck. Seats are close to the field. Many ballparks have picnic areas built between the stands along the third-base line. Some have playgrounds for toddlers and batting and pitching cages for wannabe stars. Players hang around after the game to talk to kids under a bright half-moon, maybe handing out cracked bats and signed baseballs. Entire neighborhoods sit together. People know the team's owner by his first name. Everybody knows the words to the national anthem.

The fans walk in slowly. Nobody runs or pushes. Most don't care very much if the home team wins or loses. Many don't know what level ball their team plays (AAA, AA, or A) or what league it's in. Teenage ballgirls might take batting practice with the team. The public-relations director might shag fly balls in left field during batting practice. The marketing director might also work on the grounds crew.

Minor-league ball is the baseball of the small towns and small cities, the baseball of Main Street. Everything about the minors through the years has reflected small towns, even the names of leagues, teams, and players. The big leagues have had rather rigid names, like American, National, and Federal. The minors have had marvelous names like the Evangeline, Kitty, Mink, Sally, Pony, and Copper Country Soo leagues, and briefly, in the summer of 1928, the Anthracite League, in the coal towns of Pennsylvania. Major-league teams have staid names—Yankees, Mariners, Royals—but the minors have had the Mud Hens, Sand Crabs, Clam Diggers, Homesteaders, Jobbers, River Rats, Commuters, Grizzlies, and Stogies. Major-league players have had their share of colorful nicknames— Duke, Lefty, Vinegar Bend, Red—but the minors have given us Barnacle Bill Posedel, Death Valley Scott, Bear Track Green, Bad News Galloway, Dynamite Dunn, Old

THIS FIERCE LOOKING, UNIDENTIFIED INFIELDER PLAYED FOR ALLENTOWN, PENNSYLVANIA, IN 1929.

wherever you want. The place where the game is played is always called the ballpark, never the stadium. Some parks are brand new, and some are very old. (The Durham Bulls just moved to a new ballpark, built to look old, and the old park is now home to amateur teams.) Minor-league parks

Folks Pillette, Wheezer Dell, Howitzer Moss, Bunny Brief, Six O'Clock Nelson, and Sea Lion Hall.

The minors boast Greer Park in Nashville, where the huge electronic scoreboard is shaped like a guitar; Winder Field in Little Rock, where the infield runs uphill and the outfield downhill; Redbird Stadium in Louisville, with its amusement park decor, indoor picnic area, and football grandstand; Tim McCarver Stadium in Memphis, with its artificial turf infield and real grass outfield; and old Orioles Park in Baltimore, with its maintenance shed right in the middle of left field.

The minors were first in many things. In 1914 minor leaguers were the first ballplayers to use the telegraph, sending inning-by-inning scores from the ballpark. They used permanent lights five years before the majors. They built so-called ladies' grandstands first, played the longest game in history, and went international first.

Baseball's minor leagues, never well financed like teams in the big leagues, have had a turbulent history. Leagues and teams have come and gone, some lasting just a season, some only a month. They were sometimes very popular and sometimes unpopular. During World War I and the Depression popularity plunged, but by the late 1940s there were fifty-nine leagues and 438 teams. That was the golden era for the minors, but the coming of television and other events nearly killed them, reducing their numbers to just fifteen leagues in 1963. But salvation came from the majors in the form of a deal in which they subsidized the minors in return for rights to ballplayers. In the early 1980s the minors boomed once again, with forty new ballparks and a dozen more refurbished ones and franchises popping up in state after state (there are more than 220 cities and towns with teams now).

People seem to think that it was the major leagues, with only sixteen teams until the 1950s, that made baseball the national pastime. The big leagues, and the big stars, certainly helped. But it was in the minor leagues, in rough-and-tumble Arizona mining camps and dusty small towns in Texas and tiny villages in New England and communities in Minnesota where it was so cold that pitchers would

TONY THE TIGER IS JUST ONE OF THE TRAVELING MASCOTS MINOR-LEAGUE TEAMS USE TO BUILD UP ATTENDANCE. THE FAMOUS CHICKEN, THE CAROLINA CHICKEN, AND OTHERS ALSO APPEAR FROM COAST TO COAST. KIDS LOVE THEM.

build fires in the bullpen to keep warm, that baseball truly became the national pastime.

Minor-league baseball is much the same today as it was in 1949, or 1929, or 1909. It is still the womb from which the superstars of tomorrow spring and the pasture where the old warriors fade, still a wonderful entertainment mecca for small towns like Zebulon, Yakima, Boise, Appleton, Martinsville, Johnson City, Medicine Hat, Hyannis, and Thunder Bay. It is still the game of the village green, the Fourth of July picnic, the Memorial Day parade—it is still the baseball of small-city and small-town America, the baseball of Main Street.

THIS STACK OF OLD BATS REPRESENTS 40 YEARS OF MINOR-LEAGUE PLAY.

MINOR-LEAGUE HATS BECAME A HOT COLLECTIBLE IN THE LATE 1980s.

GONE BUT NOT FORGOTTEN. ONLY THE BUFFALO BISONS REMAIN OF THESE PENNANTS COLLECTED BY FANS OVER THE PAST THIRTY YEARS. NO MORE ARE THE LYNN SAILORS, WATERBURY REDS, NEW BRITAIN RED SOX, AND HOLYOKE MILLERS.

W E DON'T LIVE NEAR A MAJOR-LEAGUE CITY. WE LIVE IN RICHMOND, AND THE BRAVES ARE OUR TEAM AND WE LOVE THEM. THEY ARE OUR YANKEES, OUR DODGERS, OUR TIGERS, ALL ROLLED INTO ONE.

—JOHN GRANT, OF RICHMOND, VIRGINIA

THIS LOWER-LEVEL MINOR-LEAGUE TEAM, SPONSORED BY HIX,
A LUMBER COMPANY, PLAYED IN A TEXAS LEAGUE IN THE 1890S.

CHAPTER ONE

IF THEY CAN DO IT, WE CAN DO IT

In the year 1876, Alexander Graham Bell invented the telephone, America's glittery Centennial Exposition was held in Philadelphia, Ulysses S. Grant, the crusty, cigar-smoking hero of the Civil War, finished his second term as president of the United States, and on a warm afternoon along the banks of the quiet Little Bighorn River in Montana, Colonel George Armstrong Custer and his Seventh Cavalry were wiped out in a pitched battle with Sioux Indians. And the National League, an association of baseball teams, was formed.

The National League was a well-organized eight-team circuit with teams only in cities with populations of seventy-five thousand or more. The Chicago White Stockings (they became the Cubs) won the 1876 pennant with a 52–14 record. The success of the National League in its first season opened the door for professional baseball at all levels, in every nook and cranny in America, wherever fathers taught sons to pitch and fans of the new pastime wolfed down hot dogs while watching a ball game.

If one well-organized league could make it, why not others? The first "minor" league was formed the next winter. Arthur "Candy" Cummings, the thin, wiry pitcher who developed the game's first curve ball and would later star in the National League himself, headed up a group of entre-preneurs, who met in Pittsburgh to develop their own league. They reasoned that if the National League could do well in large cities, another league could do just as well in smaller ones. What they needed, though, was a gimmick, something to attract a lot of press attention and make their circuit something more than just a poor man's National League. The answer was to go "international." Cummings and his partners invited teams from the Ontario cities of London and Guelph to be the Canadian (and the "international") entries in the new International Association, joining teams from Manchester, New Hampshire; Columbus, Ohio; Lynn, Massachusetts; Rochester, New York; and Pittsburgh, Pennsylvania. The teams played a short, twenty-game season, and the London Tecumsehs won the pennant the first year. The International Association expanded to ten teams the next year and played another twenty-game season. The team from Buffalo, New York, won that year's pennant.

The teams in the International Association could not pay their players full-time salaries, so games were held on weekends, allowing players to work during the week. They also booked as many nonleague games as possible, to let the players earn extra money. Buffalo, for example, played twenty league games in 1878, but played ninety-six other games against semipro, college, and amateur teams,

THE CAMDEN, NEW JERSEY, NINE, ABOUT 1885.

and even twenty-seven games against major-league teams (winning ten).

The success of the International Association intrigued just about everyone. A second minor league, the National Association, was formed in late 1877 (it absorbed the International Association in 1879), followed by the League Alliance, a thirteen-city league with teams from New York to Minneapolis. The loosely organized Northwestern League debuted in 1879 for a single season, then came back in 1882. The Eastern Championship Association was formed in 1881.

By 1882 professional baseball was gaining popularity. A new major league, the American Association, was born that year and thrived for ten years. With its success, the owners in the National, American, and minor Northwestern leagues signed an agreement prohibiting unruly raids on each other's players. Two later attempts at establishing major leagues failed: The Union Association came on the scene in 1884 and folded a year later, and the Players' League, formed by disgruntled ballplayers who felt they were underpaid, also lasted just one season, 1890.

The nation was going through great changes in the 1870s and 1880s. In the Midwest and the Northeast public schools were thriving and, in an effort to produce "complete" students, began to offer music, art, and, for physical education, baseball. These students became the first young generation of baseball fans, eager to buy tickets to games in their hometowns. With the Civil War long over and the Industrial Revolution booming, the country prospered in the 1880s. Economic ease left people with money for entertainment, such as theater, music, and baseball. It was an opportune moment for the minor leagues, which had audiences waiting with money to spend and a growing love of the game.

Since major-league baseball was restricted to just a few cities (the National League fluctuated between eight and twelve teams from 1876 to 1900), minor leagues found they could thrive in areas far from the shadows of the big-league ballparks. Minor leagues began to pop up everywhere, including parts of the country that were just beginning to flourish at the end of the nineteenth century. California's population had been booming ever since the gold rush of 1849. Settlers, arriving first by wagon train and later by railroad, also flooded Arizona, New Mexico, and Colorado, drawn at first by open land and later by cattle drives, homesteading, and silver mining. The political and economic Reconstruction that the federal government imposed on the South at the end of the Civil War ground to a halt by 1880, and Southern towns, emerging from federal restrictions, began to grow as independent communities. Leagues started in that era included the Southern League, Texas League, Connecticut State League, Iron and Oil League, Virginia League, Illinois-Indiana-Iowa League (known as the Three I League), Pennsylvania State League, Kansas State League, Hudson River League, Tri-State League, Puget Sound League, Rhode Island League, Northwestern League, Central Inter-State League, Canadian League, Utah League, Eastern Interstate League, and others. Two different leagues were in operation in Califor-

THIS SACRAMENTO CLUB PLAYED IN THE EARLY DAYS OF THE CALIFORNIA LEAGUE, ONE OF THE FIRST ORGANIZED ON THE WEST COAST. PLAYERS AND FANS OFTEN TRAVELED BACK AND FORTH TO GAMES ON RIVERBOATS.

nia by the end of the 1880s. Most of these minor leagues were loosely organized, though, and teams were by and large underfinanced, depending on local entrepreneurs whose love of the game exceeded their bank accounts. Whole leagues came and went. Some teams moved from league to league, and others, such as those from Buffalo and Rochester, played in the National League from time to time. Teams folded after a single season and sometimes in mid-season. To save money, most teams had only fifteen

GUNSLINGER WILD BILL HICKOCK WAS A BASEBALL
FAN AND IN 1872 WAS CALLED UPON, SIX-GUNS IN
HOLSTERS, TO UMPIRE A GAME IN KANSAS.

players, one serving as manager. The players would be scattered like dust throughout the league if their club collapsed. By 1898 there were twenty-one official minor leagues with more than 150 teams and another twenty or more loosely organized semiprofessional circuits. Another twenty-odd teams barnstormed from town to town.

Minor-league baseball was played in whatever facilities were available. Some small towns built bandbox stadiums that seated two to three thousand people. Other towns just put up a backstop and a wooden grandstand that could accommodate only a few hundred. Some carved fields out of public parks with grassy slopes where the fans sat. Minor-league ball grew quickly in larger, non-major-league cities, too. Baseball was so big so fast in Los Angeles that by 1899 the city had a fifteen-thousand-seat stadium for minor-league games, larger than many major-league parks.

Even in the late nineteenth century, life was still primitive and often wild in some parts of the country. Players reached towns in certain remote regions not by rail but by stagecoach and milk wagon, and rode horses to the games. Drunkenness and gambling were common in the stands in the minors throughout the 1870s and 1880s. On the field, opposing teams sometimes broke into fist-swinging melees. In 1872 a hotly contested game between two semipro teams in Kansas City, Kansas—the Antelopes and Pomeroys—ended in a riot that left dozens of players and fans injured. The two teams were scheduled to meet again a few weeks later, so local officials, fearful of an even worse bloodbath, hired Wild Bill Hickock, the legendary gunfighter and an avid baseball fan, to umpire the game wearing his six-guns. Needless to say, the game was played without incident. Afterward, the grateful city officials asked Hickock how they could repay him. After a moment of thought he asked for a new, open carriage and pair of matching snow-white horses from a nearby stable. Standing in the carriage and waving his hat in the air, Hickock drove the white horses around the town square several times to the appreciative cheers of the crowd and then, in true West tradition, rode off into the sunset.

Minor-league teams, aware that underfinanced leagues risked collapse if they didn't meet their schedules and earn needed revenue, were zealous about playing all their games. Perhaps the most dramatic illustration of their determination was the meeting on September 15, 1889, of the Western Association teams from Sioux City, Iowa, and St. Joseph, Missouri, who had just a few weeks left in their season and three rained-out games to make up. Both sides agreed to add the three makeup games to their scheduled game, making it a quadruple-header. The managers decided to make each of the three rained-out games five innings and the scheduled game seven. Because of an injury to St. Joe's catcher, third baseman Bill Krieg wound up catching all four games for his team. Sioux City swept them all, however, in a total of five hours and five minutes, leaving the team time enough to catch the evening train to Milwaukee for a game there the next day.

The minors offered endless opportunities for athletes, especially those who lived far from a city with a major-league team. Good ballplayers, crowd pleasers, could play professional ball for prestigious minor-league teams in their own cities and become local heroes or, with railroad transportation efficient and cheap by the 1880s, travel to some other town and play there. In fact, the proliferation of minor-league clubs in the 1880s created a whole new American profession—the ballplayer.

There was little money to be made in the baseball business at the minor-league level, though. An 1898 contract James Sullivan signed with the Oakland team of the California League showed that he was paid only $10 per home game and $7.50 for away games, or some $700 a year. It wasn't the money that drove young men to wield bats and steal bases in those days. It was the chance to be something special, a ballplayer.

The explosion of the minor leagues in the 1880s and 1890s also opened a window for hundreds of young men with wanderlust, who were more than willing to jump on a train and play for a minor-league team in another part of the country in pursuit of their major-league dreams. Most

THIS RARE PHOTO OF A CALIFORNIA LEAGUE GAME IN 1892 AT THE BALLPARK AT THIRTEENTH AND CENTER STREETS IN OAKLAND SHOWS THE "DUGOUT" (A LONG BENCH) AND HOW FAR THE SEATS IN LEFT FIELD WERE FROM THE FIELD.

of them were teenagers or young men away from home for the first time. On the road they could meet hundreds of new people, travel from city to city, and see places they had only read about in school. Baseball allowed them the opportunity to live out great adventures they never dreamed possible in their sleepy little towns. Perhaps no one has described the itinerant ballplayer's life better than Fred Lange, who played for Chicago and Kansas City in the Western Association in 1887 and 1888:

> Money could not buy what I learned in those years. Lincoln, Nebraska, for a mineral spring in the city, and the way we banqueted there; Chicago, for its fine lakes and fine drives; Milwaukee, for the two glasses of beer for a nickel and its beer gardens; Minneapolis, for the glass building, Lake Minnetonka, and Minnehaha Falls, where we used to gather different colored sands and put them in bottles, all colors; Sioux City, for the spring chicken we used to eat about 11 o'clock in the evening; Hastings, Nebraska, for the wind, blowing a fly ball back from the outfield to infield; Topeka, Kansas, for the Trop Hotel. . . . St. Joseph, Missouri, for the return of a ruby ring I had left at the hotel. . . . Denver, Colorado, for a train wreck we had, on leaving Denver, about nine miles out (they tell me that they have never found the engine on account of the quick-sand bottom); also for the running water in their streets; Omaha, for a snow storm on our opening game of the season, while we paraded around in hacks (I could not feel the ball when it came to me); St. Paul, for the only time in two years I was East playing base-ball that I broke the rules of the game (drinking)—the next day I could not see the ball. . . .

While people loved their hometown, minor-league heroes, they absolutely lusted after the stars of the far-distant major-league teams, the legends they read about

LUTHER TAYLOR, A DEAF-MUTE, PITCHED IN THE MAJOR LEAGUES AND LATER HURLED FOR BUFFALO.

under the thick, smudgy headlines in newspapers. In the 1880s major leaguers did not make much money either. From October first until the following March they were unemployed, and many players were forced to take menial jobs during that time. Dozens of top major-league stars quickly found two markets for themselves: winter leagues and barnstorming. Some would leave the East and take a train to California, where they would play the last two or three months of the season with the fledgling California League teams, who played into January because of the mild weather there, earning themselves another $800 or more. Luther "Dummy" Taylor, the deaf-mute pitcher for the

New York Giants, spent the winter of 1900–1901 in California, staying sharp and making extra money.

"Great weather when I was in California. Pitched well all winter. Feel tip-top now," he noted upon his return to New York for the start of the 1901 season, writing on the pad he used to communicate with his fellow players.

Other major-league players put together teams consisting of four or five players from the New York Giants, say,

THIS TRIO OF SNAPPILY DRESSED BALLPLAYERS TOILED FOR ONE OF THE TEAMS IN THE FIRST CALIFORNIA LEAGUE IN THE 1890S.

plus another ten players from California teams, mostly semipro clubs. This "New York" team would then book itself a highly hyped exhibition tour through California, which might last two or three months and provide the major leaguers with extra income, keep them in good physical shape, and, on days off, allow for a pleasant vacation in sunny California while everybody back East shoveled snow.

In 1887 four different groups of National League players headed for California. They were Jimmy Fogarty, Sandy Irwin, and Charlie Ganzel (Philadelphia); sluggers Jimmy Ryan, Fred Pfeffer, and Ed Williamson (Chicago); future Hall of Famers Buck Ewing, Roger Connor, and John Montgomery Ward (New York); and Dave Foutz, Doc Bushong, Arlie Latham, and Charley Comiskey (Chicago). Budding local stars from California teams were eager to play alongside the major leaguers because they could earn extra money and see how good they really were next to the best. Besides, defeating a team of major leaguers was a lifetime achievement. The minor leaguers all had an ulterior motive, though—playing well enough to get the major-league team to sign them or get them contracts to play in minor leagues in the East or Midwest. Although the local owners appreciated the gate money the traveling major-league teams brought in, they resented the signing of their stars without any compensation.

The major-league teams beat most of their California League opponents, but every once in awhile the locals would beat them, sending their fans into a state of euphoria. On the day after Christmas in 1887 the Pioneers, a San Francisco semipro club using some minor-league stars, beat the New York Giants, 16–8, in front of a huge crowd that overflowed onto the sidelines and into the outfield, touching off a wild celebration that lasted all night.

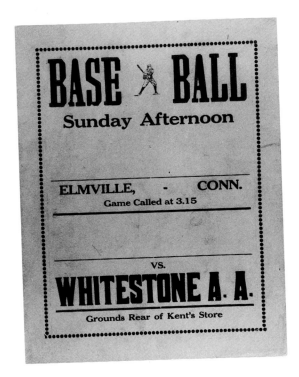

BASE BALL

Sunday Afternoon

ELMVILLE, - CONN.

Game Called at 3.15

vs.

WHITESTONE A. A.

Grounds Rear of Kent's Store

IN THE 1890S MINOR LEAGUERS OFTEN PLAYED FOR
LOCAL ATHLETIC CLUBS TO MAKE EXTRA MONEY,
USUALLY FIVE DOLLARS A GAME.

In 1897 half a dozen stars from the National League's super team, the Baltimore Orioles (which won three straight pennants in 1894, 1895, and 1896, and in 1897 finished second but won the Temple Cup in the playoffs), traveled to California. They took a team of "All Americans" with them, so fans saw not only the invincible Orioles, with stars like Hughie Jennings (later inducted in the Hall of Fame), but other National League talents, too. They booked a busy exhibition schedule that carried them up and down the coast, and nearly every single, highly promoted game was a sellout.

With its success on the major and minor circuits it is no surprise that baseball became the most popular sport on college campuses in the 1880s and 1890s. Spectators saw tremendously skilled players at college games, all the more so because some schools, very quietly, permitted minor leaguers to play on their teams. Hundreds of minor-league players earned college degrees while playing seasons for different universities. In the mid-1890s, when college teams were pulling in four to five thousand fans a game, as many as some major-league teams, several school presidents charged that some college nines had up to five minor leaguers on their starting teams. But the door swung the other way, too, as hundreds of college baseball stars earned money in the summer by playing for minor-league teams under assumed names. Since school was still in session during the first couple of months of the minor-league season, some men played for a college team and a minor-league team at the same time, then traveled with the minor-league squad full time when school was out. College teams often took the train south in the spring to warm up for their season, where they played a southern schedule against other colleges and minor-league teams. The colleges also played major-league teams just before the majors' season started, as a final tune-up for the stars.

Baseball—college, minor league, major league—became so popular that fans and players were dispirited when cold weather brought an end to the season. In the Midwest entrepreneurs began to schedule winter seasons played inside huge, drafty local military armories with high roofs. Regular leagues were established with semipro teams and teams made up of minor leaguers who had completed their seasons, and teams from different city armories would play each other in indoor series. National Guardsmen stationed at the armories also formed teams. Most armories had narrow balconies for seats and added long, wooden makeshift bleachers down below. The hard-fought games, often played as snowstorms raged outside, were high-scoring affairs, with many hits crashing off walls (a ball hit over a painted line counted as a home run). In one battle in 1891, a team in St. Paul, Minnesota, beat another with a 38–26 score.

As the minor-league teams brought baseball to every part of the nation, they also achieved a measure of integration unique in sports in heavily segregated Victorian America. Every once in a while the fans at minor-league ballparks, particularly in larger towns, would see one or two black players on the teams. The first such player was Bud Fowler, born in Cooperstown, New York, where Abner Doubleday allegedly founded baseball in 1839. Fowler played for a semipro team in New Castle, Pennsylvania, in 1872 and later for other teams. More black players appeared when the minors were formed in 1877, and by the middle of the 1880s there were more than thirty black minor-league players on teams in different circuits from New Jersey to Maine to Ohio.

Black players who integrated white minor-league teams did so by choice and by invitation. These men chose not to join any of the dozens of all-black semipro teams playing regular schedules by the late nineteenth century. Baltimore had a black league in 1874; northern Florida had one in the early 1880s; and New Orleans had a full, eight-team black minor league in the mid-1880s. In 1886 the Southern League of Colored Baseballists was formed with teams throughout the South; as a gimmick to drum up business they played with red baseballs.

In baseball's early days these pioneering black players generally had better success in the minor leagues than they did in the majors. In 1889 an all-black barnstorming team from New York called the Cuban Giants joined the Middle States League as one of its eight members. Because they were in an official minor league, the Cuban Giants' exploits were chronicled in the *Sporting Life,* a popular sports weekly of the day. At the end of the 1889 season the newspaper reported that the team had hit well over .300, led by George Williams (.371) and Sol White (.358). In 1890 the team stunned the East Coast by winning the pennant in the league (which by then was the Eastern Interstate League). There were also two black players on the Harrisburg team in that league, Frank Grant (who had a .325 average) and Clarence Williams. The Page Fence Giants, another all-black team, joined a minor league in Michigan in April 1895.

But it wasn't long before racism caught up with baseball, resulting in the segregation of major- and minor-league teams. In 1884 black catcher Moses Fleetwood Walker made it to the majors with Toledo's American Association team. The reaction to a black player in the majors was swift. Walker received death threats in several cities, and before an exhibition game with the Chicago White Stockings, Cap Anson, captain of the Chicago team (and a Hall of Famer), told the game's promoter he would take his team off the field if Walker was allowed to play. The black catcher was benched. By the end of the season, harassed mercilessly by opposing players and fans, Walker left the team. George Stovey, another black player, had become one of the top hurlers in the Eastern League, with the Newark team, in the 1880s. But Stovey's team benched him when Cap Anson threatened to pull his White Stockings off the field before an 1887 game against them. The New York Giants were interested in signing Stovey, but the politically powerful Anson reportedly quashed the deal.

In April 1887 members of the Syracuse team in the Eastern League refused to pose for a team picture if the

THE ALL-BLACK CUBAN GIANTS BARNSTORMED THE EAST COAST IN 1887 AND 1888
AND THEN TALKED THEIR WAY INTO THE MIDDLE STATES LEAGUE IN 1889.

black player on the team, Robert Higgins, appeared in it. In July 1887 the International League passed a resolution banning blacks. In September of that year the Saint Louis Browns of the American Association at the last minute refused to take the field against the Cuban Giants in a well-publicized exhibition game, infuriating seven thousand fans. In 1890, within weeks of winning the pennant in the Eastern Interstate League, the Cuban Giants were booted out. In 1896, after a little over one year, the Page Fence Giants were booted out of their league. The racial door had slammed shut. No black would play in the minors or majors again until Jackie Robinson took the field with Montreal in 1946.

By the 1890s, with three major leagues, twenty-one organized minor leagues, and hundreds of other quasi-professional teams playing short schedules or barnstorming from state to state, baseball had become the most popular sport in the country. With minor-league and semipro teams playing games several days a week and doubleheaders on weekends, the ballpark had become an entertainment mecca, providing inexpensive entertainment for millions of Americans from coast to coast. Tickets at most ballparks cost just a quarter, and trolley rides to and from the stadium a nickel. Minor-league owners were eager to build crowds and began hiring local high-school and college stars to play for their teams. They paid decent wages and could keep good players together on the same team for years. In this way they built up a local following and made the team the prized possession of a community, something the major league teams, with so much trading of players, accomplished much more rarely.

In the minors baseball was a family game from its earliest days. Every team had some kind of policy to discount kids tickets, and any kid who returned a foul ball was let in free. Everybody courted women fans, too, convinced their presence would lend the game respectability and broaden its appeal to the general public. "Ladies' Day" was started in 1887 by Abner Powell, the owner of Sportsmans' Park in New Orleans. (Powell, ever the innovator, also introduced the rain check. His greatest moment, though, came early in the 1901 season when, thoroughly frustrated by his losing team, he fired everybody. He then went through town and hired a whole new team—and suited them up in time for that afternoon's game.)

By the mid-1890s just about every ballpark had followed Powell's lead and offered a weekly Ladies' Day, when women were admitted free or for half price. Some parks built special grandstands just for women, and others had separate, aesthetically designed women's entrances to the ballpark. One built its ladies' grandstand next to a large tree down the left-field line so the women would have cool shade in the later innings. Park owners urged their friends, the sportswriters, to drum up business from women, especially from women who complained of male rowdyism. One team owner informed women fans in a flier that he had built a special bleacher "especially for the ladies, from which they may view the game without being annoyed by the noisy crowd." The *Austin Statesman* wrote on June 24, 1889: "Don't fear to compromise your sex by attending the baseball game. It is affirmed on the best authority that Mrs. Cleveland [wife of the President] is enthusiastically devoted to the game. That should make it fashionable and insure the game financial success in Texas."

Communities planned their weekends around their team's schedule. People would make a day of it, arriving at the ballpark early for a picnic before the game, watching the game in the afternoon, and perhaps going out to dinner or off to visit friends afterwards. People in small cities and rural towns began to see the team not only as the community's entertainment, but as an extension of themselves, reveling in its wins and wallowing in its losses. When Utica beat Wilkes-Barre in the New York State League, it was a victory for the whole town of Utica, not just for the team. The teams in minor-league cities began to represent the fortunes of their hometowns. "Salt Lake has for a number of years fostered the game of baseball," wrote an editor of the *Salt Lake Tribune* in 1887. "In fact, our city would not be up in modern ideas did she not do so. In these times, baseball clubs are almost an imperative necessity."

Newspapers in small cities helped minor-league ball thrive. During the 1880s more and more sports stories began to appear in print, and in the mid-1890s the Hearst newspaper chain started the first regular sports sections. In 1892 the *Sporting News*, a weekly devoted to baseball, both major and minor league, was started in Saint Louis and within three years had an unheard of circulation of sixty thousand. By 1887 there were enough sportswriters to form the first chapter of the Baseball Reporters Association of America. Stores began to use ball game illustrations in their newspaper advertisements, and the papers themselves began printing elaborate schedules for the local minor-league team.

By the turn of the century the minor leagues, with teams in cities and villages throughout the country—compared with the scattered, relatively few teams of the majors—had made baseball something more than sport: They had made it the national pastime.

The minors reached a crossroads at the turn of the century, victims of their own success. The different teams and leagues managed to develop and showcase outstanding hitters, pitchers, and fielders. Local newspapers ballyhooed their achievements. Thousands flocked to their tiny ballparks to see them play. Everybody soon knew about these stars, including major-league managers and scouts. They raided the minors constantly and snagged the best players, be they young sluggers new to the game or seasoned players who, after many years on the team, had become part of the community. Towns and small cities were often outraged when major-league teams snatched their players away. Clark Griffith, who went on to a long and illustrious career as the owner of the Washington Senators, was an outstanding and revered pitcher for six seasons with the Milwaukee Brewers of the Western League and then with teams in the Pacific Northwest League. Then the Saint Louis Browns signed him and took him away to the majors. Jack Chesbro, who would become the only man to pitch forty winning games in the majors, was a star pitcher for Richmond, Virginia, in the Atlantic League, for three seasons (winning twenty-three games in 1898) before he was spirited away by the Pittsburgh Pirates in 1899. Word about good minor leaguers spread so fast they were sometimes hijacked after a single season, as happened to Wee Willie Keeler ("Hit 'em where they ain't . . ."), who hit .373 in his very first season with Binghamton, New York, in the Eastern League, and was then snatched by the Baltimore

Orioles (he went on to the Hall of Fame). The players, realizing their dreams of playing in the majors, were of course delighted. The minor-league team owners, though, were furious. They received no compensation for the lost player, whom they "owned" via a contract.

Year after year the raiding of the minors continued, but it reached a crescendo in 1901. Ban Johnson, the former sports columnist who became president of the Western League, was convinced he could successfully challenge the National League. In 1901, his brand-new American League, with teams in Baltimore, Washington, Cleveland, Milwaukee, Chicago, Boston, Detroit, and Philadelphia, opened its gates. To get players, these new major-league clubs raided existing National League teams and launched a full-scale invasion of the minors, signing more than 150 players from across the country. Now being pummeled by two large and rich leagues, the minor-league owners were convinced that with their star gate attractions gone, they would soon be out of business.

Finally, seeing that there was strength in numbers and even more strength in lawyers, in 1901 the heads of seven large minor leagues—Eastern, Western, New York State, Three I (Illinois-Indiana-Iowa), Western Association, Pacific Northwest, and New England—with proxy letters of support from several others, met in Chicago. They formed the National Association to represent themselves and fight the raiders from the major leagues. They also organized themselves into leagues on different levels of talent to prevent some of the runaway games that bored fans. Teams would now play in four classifications: A, B, C, and D, with A representing the best teams. Fans would now know what to expect. More permanent schedules were put in place and a tighter reserve clause was drawn up to prevent players from jumping from one minor-league team to another, as many had done in the 1890s. Salary caps were also imposed to prevent teams from luring ballplayers with the promise of more money (no team in the Western Canada League, for example, could pay any player more than $1,800 a year). Most important, they told the major-league teams bluntly that they would no longer release any of their players without compensation, and that any efforts to take even one more player would result in costly lawsuits. It was war.

The two major leagues, knowing they needed the minors as a talent pool, kicked and screamed. But by the start of the 1903 season they entered into an agreement with the minors that called for payment of up to $7,500 to the minor-league club for any player signed to a major-league contract.

That agreement (payment for players gave the minors a whole new source of revenue), plus the success of the new schedules and reserve clause, sent the minor leagues into the twentieth century as the largest and most successful sports organization in America.

THESE BALLPLAYERS WERE PHOTOGRAPHED AT ONE OF THE VERY FIRST MINOR-LEAGUE OLD TIMERS' DAYS, IN 1897, IN IRVINGTON, NEW JERSEY. THE OCCASION WAS A REUNION OF THE TEAM THAT HAD PLAYED THE FABLED CINCINNATI RED STOCKINGS OF 1869.

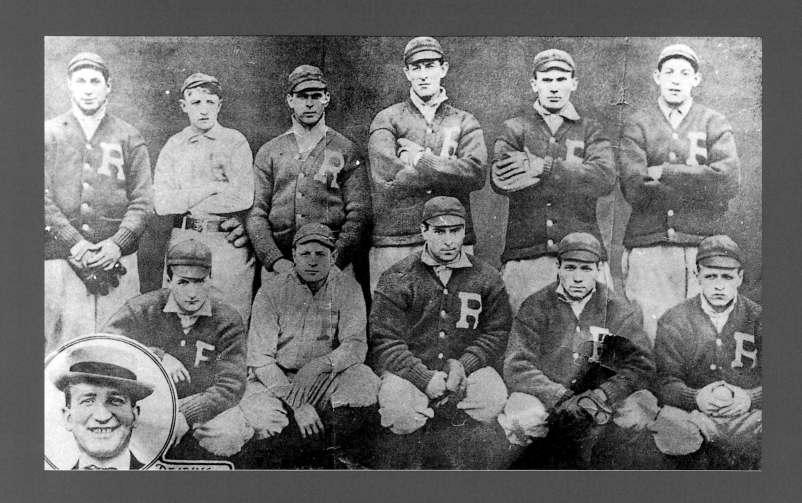

The Reading Pretzels of 1910, owned by William Yeitzel (inset), played against teams from small towns in Pennsylvania and New Jersey.

CHAPTER TWO

MINOR LEAGUES AND MAJOR SUCCESS

Reading, Pennsylvania, lies deep in the rolling hills of iron-ore country. It is a typical small American city, steeped in history and tradition. Like so many towns, it is built around a lovely green park dotted with statues of a Civil War regiment, President William McKinley, and the local volunteer fire department. George Washington is said to have slept at its Federal Inn, and Hessian soldiers, captured when Washington crossed the Delaware, were held prisoner there. The town grew when the Schuylkill and Union Canals were finished in the 1820s, connecting it to Philadelphia to the southeast and other cities to the west. It was later connected to the rest of the country by railroad. In its heyday it thrived on the iron-ore industry and was jammed with steelworks, rolling mills, and machine shops. Workers were blue collar. Unemployment was extremely low.

Business was so good that in 1909—the year the Reading Pretzels were fighting their way through the Tri-State League against Altoona, Lancaster, and Harrisburg—Reading produced ore and factory products worth over $35 million. On their days off mill workers took their families, laden with blankets and baskets of food, to picnics on the banks of the Schuylkill or in the city park, rode bikes along the canals, fished lazily in the town's rivers, or jammed the ballpark to see the Pretzels take on their Tri-State League rivals.

The scene in Reading was typical of America, and of baseball, in the early years of the new century. The formation of the National Association of minor leagues and the agreement they reached not only solidified the existing leagues, including the Tri-State, but sent a clear signal across the country that the minors were going to be more stable, better organized, and better financed, and would provide more and finer baseball for their fans. Leagues would continue to play independently but now they had an umbrella group to represent, protect, and unite them. The agreement could not have been reached at a more opportune time, for the new century kicked off a wonderful new era in baseball, an era in which hundreds of new minor-league teams began play and the major leagues flourished, bringing more attention to baseball at all levels than at any time in history.

In 1903, after the two major leagues worked out their own differences, the first World Series was played. Boston, of the American League, beat Pittsburgh, of the National League. At the same time, the era saw the emergence of some of the game's all-time greats: Christy Mathewson, Joe McGinnity, Ty Cobb, Walter Johnson, Three-Finger Brown, Home Run Baker, the Cubs' double-play combination of Joe Tinker, Johnny Evers, and Frank Chance, and managers Wilbert Robinson, John McGraw, and

Connie Mack. Crude old wooden stadiums were knocked down and replaced with concrete stadiums such as the Polo Grounds (New York City), Wrigley Field (Chicago), Crosley Field (Cincinnati), and Shibe Park (Philadelphia). Pulp magazines debuted and, targeting a teenage boy market, flooded their pages with baseball stories about characters like Frank Merriwell. Baseball novels for kids appeared ("Baseball Joe" was one of the most popular characters), and in many of them the young hero worked his way up to a position with a minor-league ball club. This passage from a 1909 best-seller, *The Shortstop*, set in a minor league, is typical:

> Poke's heart swelled in his throat, as could be seen by the way he swallowed. He was white and dripping with sweat. His perturbation was so manifest that the Toledo players jeered at him. His situation then was the most important and painful stage in the evolution of a pitcher. Much depended on how he would meet it. He threw the ball toward the next batter, who hit it back at him. Poke made a good stop of the ball, dropped it, recovered it, and then stood helpless. Both runners were safe. The Toledo players yelled; the bleachers roared.

Sound authentic? It should. The author was none other than Zane Grey, the fabled writer of Westerns, who was a pitcher in the Inter-State League in Ohio at the turn of the century and played minor-league ball until he sold his first novel.

Advances in printing technology allowed newspapers to produce wonderful black-and-white photographs on their pages. By 1910 sports sections splattered pictures of ballplayers and their games all over their pages, giving baseball phenomenal publicity and attracting droves of fans. Small-town papers, with no major-league teams to call their own, inundated their readers with stories and photos of the local minor-league club.

The boom in the majors after the creation of the American League in 1901 fueled the boom in the minors. Between 1902 and 1906 alone, ten new leagues with a total of eighty teams debuted, with such names as the Kitty League (Kentucky-Illinois-Tennessee) and the Mink League (Missouri-Iowa-Nebraska-Kansas). By 1914 the thirst for baseball in small cities and towns was so great that forty-two leagues, with more than three hundred teams, were playing in the minors. The minors linked together small cities and towns across America, bringing baseball to burgs far from the concrete canyons of New York and the wharves of Boston. Towns and small cities all over the country were as proud of their thriving minor-league teams as people in Chicago and New York were of their big-league clubs.

The minor leagues, of course, never considered themselves minor. At the start of the century, long before the advent of television brought major-league baseball to every town in America, the minor-league teams were the "major" baseball attraction in their area of the country. Their games were as lively as those in the big leagues, sometimes more so. In what might have been the wildest minor-league game ever played, tiny Corsicana, in the Texas League, beat Texarkana 51–3 in 1902. The Corsicana batters hit twenty-one home runs, drove in forty-five runs on fifty-three hits, and had twenty-one doubles or triples. The star for Corsicana was Nig Clarke, who went to the plate eight times and hit eight home runs. He wasn't alone. Player-manager Dave O'Connor had seven hits, and Bill Alexander and Ike Pendleton each collected six. It was the most lopsided win in the history of baseball, and the strangest

THE MINNEAPOLIS JOURNAL LEASED THE COVETED SCOREBOARD AT
NICOLLET PARK TO LET PEOPLE KNOW WHERE THEY COULD READ ABOUT THE
TEAM. HERE, A BRASS BAND PLAYS AS BOTH TEAMS GATHER FOR THE
TRADITIONAL OPENING-DAY FLAG RAISING.

THE RATHER WILD LOOKING POINT ISABEL, TEXAS, TARPONS PLAYED IN A LOWER MINOR LEAGUE IN 1911. THE
TEAM'S HEADQUARTERS WAS THE JUAN SIMO SALOON (THEY ARE POSED HERE ON ITS FRONT PORCH).

part of it was that Texarkana's manager, wanting to show confidence in his starting pitcher, Bill DeWitt, left him in for the whole game. When criticized by reporters for his performance, the manager pulled out the box score and noted proudly that he had walked only three.

The minors had plenty of other spectacular moments.

In 1911 center fielder Walter Carlisle, of Los Angeles, a circus acrobat in the off-season, raced in to spear a line drive just behind second base as the runners on first and second, certain it was a single, took off. He somersaulted once, touched second for the force, and ran down the runner trying to get back to first for a rare, unassisted triple play. On

May 23, 1911, a wobbly rookie named Jim Parks started his first game for Richmond, Kentucky, and threw a no-hitter. Fred Toney, who would throw a no-hitter in the majors, warmed up by tossing a seventeen-inning no-hitter for Winchester, Kentucky, in 1917. Harry Hedgepethe, of Petersburg, Virginia, went him one better by pitching a no-hitter in the first game of a doubleheader and then

LOUISVILLE MANAGER JACK HAYDEN TAKES A SWING WITH CATCHER TUBBY CLEMONS BEHIND HIM IN 1910 STYLE. ANY PLAYER WHO HIT THE HUGE BULL DURHAM TOBACCO BILLBOARD WAS PAID TWENTY-FIVE DOLLARS BY THE COMPANY.

OPENING DAY IN MINOR-LEAGUE CITIES WAS A MAJOR EVENT FOR THE POPULACE. MAYOR ROBERT WILL OF LOUISVILLE, KENTUCKY, THREW OUT THE FIRST BALL OF THE 1910 SEASON AS LOCAL SLUGGER NICK CULLOP WATCHED.

throwing a one-hitter in the second. In the 1906 season Memphis Chicks pitcher Glen Liebhardt won thirty-six games, ten of them by pitching both ends of five doubleheaders. In 1903 tiny Kingston, New York, of the Hudson River League, became the first American professional baseball team to tour Cuba, when it raised enough money in town to spend the winter in the Caribbean. (The Cincinnati Reds of the National League would become the

No opening day got started without the raising of the flag, hoisted here amid a forest of beer signs at the Sacramento ballpark in 1906.

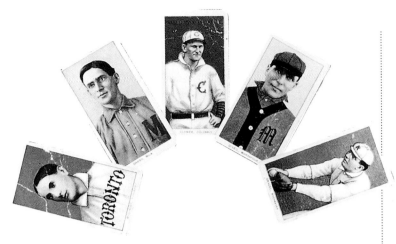

THE MINOR LEAGUES WERE SO STRONG AROUND THE TURN OF THE CENTURY THAT TOBACCO COMPANIES SLIPPED CARDS OF MINOR LEAGUERS AS WELL AS MAJOR LEAGUERS INTO CIGARETTE PACKS.

first major-league team to play in the Caribbean, but not until five years later.)

But even in those halcyon days minor-league baseball had its less than shining moments. Then, as now, everybody harassed the umpires. In 1904 the president of the Louisville, Kentucky, team got so angry at an umpire after a loss that he threw the ump's clothes into the street and locked him out of his dressing room. In 1905 police in Newark, New Jersey, had to be called in to escort an umpire out of a stadium during a riot when the home team lost. In 1924 Alabama Jones, a player from Muskogee, Oklahoma, was suspended for kicking an umpire in a dispute and ordered to pay his medical bills. Just two weeks later that ump himself was suspended for challenging a fan to a fistfight in the middle of a game. A Dubuque, Iowa, newspaper ran this item on July 9, 1910: "Clem Sheridan, the famous American League umpire, has quit because his eyes are going bad. He ought to come to this league where it is a habit and not an affliction."

The country was wild about baseball in the early days of this century. Looking back to those years, lifelong baseball fan W. W. Busby, of Hernando, Mississippi, wrote in the *Memphis* (Tennessee) *Commercial Appeal* newspaper in 1976: "Memphis and the surrounding country were baseball crazy in 1901. Every neighborhood in Memphis had a kid team that played and fought all summer. We wore black satin shirts with 'Swind Sluggers' (a local blacksmith shop) sewed in white letters by our mothers. We were ten and eleven years old. I don't remember whether we won any games or lost any, but I recall that we did not lose a fight."

General stores would sponsor games played in fields next to them, and in the off-season sporting-goods stores would hastily contact all the minor leaguers living in the area to get together games that would draw a thousand or more people. The demand for baseball in California any day of the year was so great that one minor leaguer got this note on December 17, 1906, from the owner of A. E. Hawley Sporting Goods, in Santa Ana:

Dear Friend,
Lester Slalback wishes me to write you that there will be a game of ball Christmas Day at 2:00 P.M. and that he wants you to come. We can get a large crowd. And the plan is to turn over half of the gate receipts to the players. So all will get something and, the more the players interest themselves in getting a crowd, the more they will get. Be sure to come. We want to keep the interest up.

Yours truly,
A. E. Hawley

Schedules for 1908 show that thirty minor leagues were operating from coast to coast, with teams in large cities

Y, MARCH 23, 1910.   3

IN 1910 THE ANHEUSER-BUSCH COMPANY RAN THIS
SERIES OF CARTOON ADS IN LOCAL PAPERS IN MINOR-
LEAGUE CITIES TO TIE IN TO THE OPENING OF THE SEASON.

such as San Francisco, Milwaukee, Baltimore, Toronto, New Orleans, and Atlanta, and in small towns such as New Bedford, Massachusetts, and New Castle, Pennsylvania. Among the leagues were the Northeast Arkansas League, which had teams in such burgs as Caruthersbie, Paragould, Jonesboro, and Blytheville, and the Illinois-Missouri League, with thriving little franchises in Pekin, Clinton, Canton, and Lincoln. There were so many teams in Wisconsin that it took two leagues to hold them: The Wisconsin-Illinois League had teams in Fond du Lac and Oshkosh, and the Wisconsin-Minnesota League had nines in La Crosse and Eau Claire. Western Canada had teams in cities like Calgary, Edmonton, and Winnipeg, as well as in towns such as Moose Jaw and Medicine Hat. The best players in the minor-league teams went on to the ma-

jors, but they were quickly replaced by hundreds of others just out of high school or off college campuses, eager to play in the minors for awhile until someone made room for them in the big leagues.

With mass production putting automobiles within the reach of the middle class, Americans were increasingly mobile and began flocking in greater numbers to the ballparks of minor-league towns to see games. By 1915 railroad lines connected most towns, big and small, and riverboats connected many others. Hundreds of fans would pile onto a train or boat and follow their hometown minor-league team to an out-of-town game.

Teams tacked up large cardboard broadsides throughout towns to let people know when the next game was. Newspapers printed schedules of games, and department stores handed out flyers with sale advertisements printed on one side and team baseball schedules on the other. Each spring, stores in small cities featured baseball illustrations in their newspaper ads, usually along with some supportive slogan. Players were paid to make personal appearances at stores and for their portraits in newspaper ads.

In the days before radio, small-town newspapers would erect large boards next to their offices where copyboys

THOUSANDS OFTEN GATHERED OUTSIDE NEWSPAPER OFFICES OR DEPARTMENT STORES THAT MOUNTED ELECTRIC SCOREBOARDS TO SHOW FANS THE BATTER-BY-BATTER MOVEMENT IN THE WORLD SERIES OR MINOR-LEAGUE PLAYOFF SERIES.

WITH A SMILE THAT WIDE, THIS GUY MUST HAVE WON BIG. HE'S THE OPERATOR OF A BETTING PARLOR. ON THE WALL, UNDER THE LIGHT, YOU CAN SEE THE MINOR- AND MAJOR-LEAGUE GAMES SCHEDULED THAT DAY.

BALLPLAYERS DRESSED WELL AT THE TURN OF THE CENTURY. THIS
GROUP COULD PASS FOR UNIVERSITY PROFESSORS, BUT THEY WERE
ACTUALLY A SMALL-TOWN SEMIPRO BALL TEAM FROM DAVENPORT, IOWA.

would post inning-by-inning scores of league games as they came in via telephone, while fans stood by and watched. Ray McKinley, a nineteen-year-old entrepreneur, rented the roof of the first movie theater in Fort Worth, Texas, in 1906 and put up his own scoreboard, which posted inning-by-inning scores of all games in the Texas League. McKinley paid $9 a week for the phone reports and charged $175 a month for the advertising space next to the scores. Throughout America, movie theaters used gongs or whistles to let silent-movie audiences know what was going on at the ballpark. In 1908 one Texas theater had to stop the film when mayhem broke out after the home team bashed five home runs in one inning. In 1914 a ballpark in Memphis sent the first inning-by-inning game reports via telegraph—to fans aboard paddle-wheeler cruises on the Mississippi River. By 1918 it was common practice for towns to erect huge electric scoreboards on the roofs of buildings in Main Street business districts that indicated hits, strikeouts, fly balls, and runs within seconds after the telegraph report came in. Police in minor-league cities often had to shut down business districts during league championships.

In the minors it was important for teams to play all games, regardless of the weather. In the 1890s many teams had gone out of business because they missed so many games that fans no longer showed up when they did play. In the early 1900s the game was often played no matter how many people were in the stands. On November 8, 1905, a cold, stormy day in Portland, Oregon, two Pacific Coast League teams insisted on going ahead with a game that should have been rained out. Only one fan showed up to watch (and did not even move to a better seat!). It was common practice in those days, before public-address systems, for the umpire, equipped with a large megaphone,

WALTER JOHNSON, THE HALL OF FAME SENATORS HURLER, WAS ONE OF MANY SUPERSTARS, LIKE BABE RUTH AND LOU GEHRIG, WHO PITCHED FOR LOCAL SEMIPRO TEAMS IN MINOR-LEAGUE BALLPARKS ON HIS DAYS OFF.

to announce the two starting lineups to the crowd. He always sonorously intoned: "Ladies and gentlemen, today's lineups are. . . ." That rainy day all the players, owners, and umpires went about business as usual, with one change. When the umpire took the megaphone and looked up at the single man in the seats, he changed his address and began, "Sir, today's lineups are. . . ." And the game was played.

THE BEARDED HOUSE OF DAVID TEAM BARNSTORMED THROUGHOUT THE
UNITED STATES, PLAYING MANY MINOR-LEAGUE TEAMS IN EXHIBITIONS.

The great boom in baseball in the early twentieth century provided opportunities to minorities who would otherwise have remained well outside mainstream society. Several Native Americans, for instance, had fine careers in the minors. Some, such as Charley Bender and John Myers (both were immediately nicknamed "Chief"), were so good they made it to the majors. James Smith, who picked up the nickname Bluejacket, became a pitcher in the Three I (Illinois-Iowa-Indiana) League in 1912, winning 24 games. He pitched for different teams, including a Federal League team, for seven seasons. An even better Native American pitcher was Louis Leroy, a Seneca who attended the Carlisle School for Indians at the turn of the century and was 13-5 in his first season with Buffalo, in the Eastern League. LeRoy went on to win 239 games in an impressive seven-league, eighteen-year career that included two month-long stints with the Yankees and capped it with an 18–6 record in his final season. Jim Thorpe, the great track and field star and All-American football player, was another Carlisle graduate who played minor-league ball between semesters, which cost him his Olympic medals (later restored). He had a decent, six-year career with the New York Giants from 1913 to 1919, with stints in the minors at Jersey City and Harrisburg in 1914–15. He returned to play in the minors right through 1928 (he played football in the brand new National Football League in the fall, baseball in summer). A professional team of Seneca players in New York played a forty- to sixty-game schedule against semipro and minor-league teams in the Northeast between 1900 and 1920.

Semiprofessional baseball, a crazy mix of minor-league and town ball, also became wildly popular after the turn of the century. Baseball was born with town ball, games between amateur teams whose players were all from the same community. Although they were amateurs, they often passed the hat so the players could go home with a few dollars for their efforts. By the early 1900s, though, entrepreneurs began to realize that America's thirst for baseball was practically unquenchable. By 1908 there were two major leagues with sixteen teams and thirty minor leagues with 214 teams playing coast to coast. Even so, thousands of towns and cities did not have professional baseball. Fans today think nothing of driving 120 miles on a superhighway to see a major-league game, but in 1908, even with the newfangled automobile, people couldn't easily travel more than a few miles from home to anywhere that was not on a railroad line.

Semipro teams began to appear at the turn of the century to fill the void. A local town would support a team of its own, paying the players a seasonal salary and/or a fee of five to twenty dollars per game. The team would play other semipro teams in the county or state. These games were big events, especially in rural areas, where two-hour-long picnics often preceded a semipro game, usually a Sunday doubleheader, and ad hoc band concerts often followed them. On the Fourth of July in 1913, there were four semipro doubleheaders going on at the same time in Lima, Ohio, all preceded by picnics. The annual county fair in Sussex, New Jersey, included a doubleheader baseball game on the Fourth of July, while just down the road in Newton, the Texaco Barons, a team sponsored by a local gas station, played another doubleheader.

Most major cities had their own semipro city leagues in addition to major-league franchises. The city leagues would consistently draw from four to eight thousand fans a game. Semipro teams in Cincinnati were so successful they had to rent the Reds' ballpark to accommodate their crowds, while across the state, Cleveland alone had twelve semipro leagues in 1907. In the 1930s Dexter Park, a single-tier, fifteen-thousand-seat stadium, was built in the borough of Queens in New York City as the new home of the Bushwicks, a semipro team as talented as many minor-league clubs. The stadium was often filled to capacity.

Semipro teams thrived because they offered good baseball and gave locals a chance to see up-and-coming stars and future major leaguers. John McGraw, future manager of the New York Giants, got his start playing semipro ball for five dollars a game; Casey Stengel played on a barnstorming semipro team for a dollar a day; and Christy Mathewson, later a star for the Giants, earned twenty-five bucks a day in a semipro league. A young Dwight D. Eisenhower played semipro ball under an assumed name in the summer of 1910, earning ten dollars a day. A few major

PLAYERS PITCHED IN TO KEEP FIELDS IN SHAPE.

leaguers would walk off their teams after disputes, work out deals with semipro teams, and play entire seasons, earning as much as they did in the major leagues. Their names on marquees would double and triple crowds for the semipro games. Johnny Kling, a famous Chicago Cubs catcher who took a leave from baseball during the 1909 season as he successfully chased the world billiard championship, earned $4,500 for a Kansas City semipro team that summer, equal to his Cubs pay.

Beginning around 1905 and continuing through the 1940s, semipro teams, especially those in towns far from big cities whose fans never got a chance to see the superstars, made a practice of hiring major-league players to join their team in a single game. Walter Johnson often pitched on his days off for semipro teams that would meet his price: $500 per game. Babe Ruth was a frequent semipro "ringer," playing for anyone for $500 to $700 a game. Lou Gehrig played regularly for a semipro team in Morristown, New

Jersey (in one game in Boonton, New Jersey, he hit an out-of-the-park home run that two fans reportedly measured off at six hundred feet). Satchel Paige, the star pitcher of the Negro Leagues, earned so much money playing for different semipro teams (up to $30,000 a year) that he bought his own plane to fly from town to town.

The markets for baseball seemed infinite early in the century, and promoters soon started sending touring teams across the country to cash in on the nation's appetite for the sport. As early as 1900 Connie Mack, later the long-time manager of the Philadelphia A's, organized an all-star minor-league team in the Midwest (he managed the Milwaukee Brewers at the time) and sent them on a national tour. The All Nations team, with ballplayers from different countries, toured as early as 1912. The Mohawk Giants of Schenectady, New York, an all-black team, played more than two hundred games a year on its national tours in the 1920s, as did the Kansas City Monarchs of the Negro League and the House of David, a team sponsored by a Michigan religious sect (all the players wore long beards). The Indianapolis Clowns, an all-black team started by Abe Saperstein, who later founded the Harlem Globetrotters, played a two-hundred-game schedule that mixed baseball and comedy. College players used fake names and barnstormed to make extra money. The Hogansburg Indians, a squad of Native Americans who were students at Carlisle, the Native American college in Pennsylvania (Jim Thorpe may have played for them), traveled the Northeast at the turn of the century, playing minor-league teams.

Most of the thousands of semipro teams across the United States and Canada were made up of young men who just wanted to play baseball. For most of them, the twenty or thirty dollars they received per game was more than enough because they were convinced they could parlay their experience into a stint with the minor leagues and then, given a chance there, the majors. They hoped at each game that scouts were somewhere in the grandstand, watching them. If the scouts failed to find them, they sometimes acted as their own agents. The manager of a team in the Western League received this letter from a player on a semipro team in Morse, Saskatchewan, sent from the hotel where he lived:

July 11, 1911

Dear Friend,

I drop you a line in regards of a position playing on your ball team. I am catching for the Morse team but they don't play steady and I've been watching the Western League and think that's the place for me, so if you give me a chance I'll try and show you what I can do in the line of baseball. I come from Pittsburgh, Pa., and played on some fast teams there, so I'll thank you for anything that you will do for me. Goodbye.

Yours in good sports.
Wm. Borden
Morse Sask. Player

PS: I can play third base, also.

There were more than a thousand semipro teams by 1915, enough for a national organization, the National Baseball Federation, and a national championship. The championship game underlined the popularity of semipro ball, attracting a hundred thousand fans to Brookside, a natural grass-bowl stadium in Cleveland. Semipro teams began to pull in not just trophies but money, too. In the mid-1930s the various national championships were awarding $5,000 in prize money, which amounted to some $300 per player, a hefty sum at the height of the Depression. Even at the lowest community levels, townsmen found that they could earn extra revenue playing ball, and that drove more and more good high school and college players to join semipro teams. The average weekly salary for blue-collar workers in the United States in the 1930s was just seventy-five dollars a week, so another forty bucks from two ball games a week over five months' time (in cash and thus easy to hide from Uncle Sam) could pay a lot of bills. Some teams, eager to make as much money as possible, booked two concurrent schedules using two different names. In 1942 a New York team played one entire seventy-game season as the Bronx All Stars and another seventy-game season on their nights off as the Allentown Red Sox.

Everyone knows how good Satchel Paige and Johnny Kling were, but how good were the rest of the semipros? Some were just good former high school stars who couldn't

> I STARTED GOING TO SEE THE LOUISVILLE TEAM IN THE SUMMER OF 1919, WHEN I WAS SEVEN. THERE WAS A CRACKED PIECE OF WOOD AT THE BOTTOM OF THE FENCE AT ECLIPSE PARK BEHIND THE FIRST BASE SIDE. YOUR BUDDY WOULD OPEN IT UP AND YOU'D SLIDE UNDER AND THEN YOU'D HOLD IT OPEN FROM THE INSIDE AND HE'D SLIDE UNDER. HUNDREDS OF KIDS GOT TO SEE THE TEAM THAT WAY EVERY DAY. THEY'D ANNOUNCE THE ATTENDANCE AND THE OWNER WOULD LOOK AROUND AND SEE TWICE AS MANY PEOPLE THERE, HALF OF WHOM SLID UNDER THAT FIRST BASE FENCE.
> —ROBERT PIERCE, OF LOUISVILLE, KENTUCKY

LARRY SUTTON
1878-1934

LARRY SUTTON WAS ONE OF THE COUNTRY'S BEST TALENT SCOUTS. DURING 1918 AND 1919 HE FOUND CASEY STENGEL, AMONG OTHERS, IN THE MINORS AND BROUGHT THEM UP FOR BROOKLYN.

go any further in baseball. But some were superb. In 1901 the Memphis team of the semipro Southern Association beat three major-league teams in exhibitions—but was upended by a semipro team from tiny (population 750) Friars Point, Mississippi. New York's Bushwicks, in a much-hyped challenge, beat the Brooklyn Dodgers, 2–1, in 1916. The Greenwich Village (New York) Hurons were undermined by their own success, forced to disband in the summer of 1942 after five of their starters were drafted by the majors and sent to play on minor-league teams.

The minor leagues flourished in the last era of innocence, the days before World War I, because of simple economics. They generated moderate revenues through ticket sales and kept overhead costs down with small stadiums and office staffs and, most effectively, by maintaining bare-bones pay-

rolls. They employed only twelve to fifteen players, with one serving as manager, to save money. In the year 1915 most minor leaguers were earning around $800 for a six-month season (major leaguers earned about $3,000) and had to work full-time jobs in the off-season to match the salary of the average American worker. Owners were not obliged to pay higher wages, because reserve clauses in their contracts bound the players to them. They also knew that young men would rather earn $800 playing baseball than mining ore or shoveling coal—and that the minors were a springboard to the majors, a lure few young ballplayers could resist. What did it matter if a player made just $800 for one or two summers? During the twenty summers after that he would earn untold thousands as a major-league star, live in a mansion, appear on the cover of *Baseball Magazine,* and drive around in a long touring car, right? Trying to make ends meet, minor-league players argued with owners for more money each and every year. They sometimes had to take salary cuts and then had to work moonlighting jobs while they played or tried to get their wives or girlfriends jobs at the ballpark. They often lived three and four to a room in a boardinghouse, forgoing such nonessentials as new clothes. In the off-season they played winter baseball in the Caribbean or ran baseball schools for kids.

The trials and tribulations of Heinie Henricks, a minor-league pitcher from California who played in Canada at the start of the century, were typical of the financial ups and downs of minor-league ballplayers trying to scratch out a living with a bat and glove. A batch of recently discovered letters describes his yearly frustrations at trying to make the big leagues.

On March 17, 1910, W. E. Morrow, the new manager of Henricks's Brandon, Manitoba, team in the Western

Canada League, wrote him to clear up a financial problem. It was the first of Henricks's many financial run-ins with different clubs, a scenario typical of minor-league ball of that era: "My attention was called to the fact that there is some differences between you and the club. If this is true I want to straighten it for if we are going to work together this season I want everything satisfactory on your part and on the part of the Brandon Club. Please state the trouble and believe me I will do my best to fix matters up."

On June 22, 1912, writing to J. H. Farrell, president of the Western Canada League, Henricks outlined a problem still lingering from the 1911 season:

> During the season of 1911, I was the property of the Brandon Base-Ball Club, in the Western Canada League. On July 15, I received salary up to date. On August 10, whilst on the road, I was traded to the Edmonton Club. Manager Luster of the Brandon club wired W. T. Weatherstone, president of the Brandon club, to forward me a cheque from July 16 to August 9, inclusive, at the rate of $150 per month. The check was never forwarded. About August 20, the Brandon club dropped out of the league. Have I any chance of collecting the money, without appealing to court?

Another league officer, Fred Johnston, wrote back that since Brandon had dropped out, Henricks would not get his pay. The next season Henricks, apparently a good ballplayer, had two invitations: a contract with the Edmonton club that included a salary cut and allowed him to work on his days off, and a deal to play in San Diego that included provisions for room, board, salary, and of all things, income from a refreshment stand.

Henricks received the following from the Edmonton team, dated April 9, 1913:

When Mackin [club president] sent you the February 1st contract, we did not know that the salary limit would be reduced. However, to make a long story short about the best we can offer you is $135 [per month] and transportation to Edmonton . . . and home again, providing you finish the season with us and carry us to victory in at least half your games. Ford has accepted a cut of about 30 percent and Clayton, if he plays at all, has agreed to a cut of 20 percent. In addition to this, we

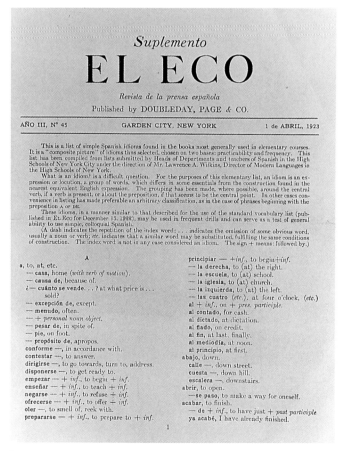

JUST ABOUT ALL THE BALLPLAYERS HEADED FOR WINTER BALL IN THE CARIBBEAN PURCHASED *EL ECO*, A HANDY SPANISH-ENGLISH TRANSLATION BOOKLET. HUNDREDS OF MINOR LEAGUERS MADE EXTRA MONEY PLAYING BASEBALL ON CARIBBEAN ISLANDS AND IN SOUTH AMERICA.

SOME WEALTHY OWNERS SPARED NO EXPENSE AND SENT
PLAYERS TO SPRING TRAINING ON CRUISE SHIPS.

SETTING SAIL BY STEAMSHIP FOR FLORIDA
AND SPRING TRAINING.

A TRIP TO THE BEACH
NEAR THE BALLPARK WAS
ALMOST MANDATORY.
HERE THE NEWARK, NEW
JERSEY, BEARS TEST THE
WARM FLORIDA WATERS.

SEVERAL MINOR-
LEAGUE TEAMS
STAYED AT THE
LAVISH PONCE DE
LEON HOTEL IN
SAINT AUGUSTINE,
FLORIDA, DURING
SPRING TRAINING.

THIS SMALL BUT SERVICEABLE BALLPARK IN SAINT
AUGUSTINE, FLORIDA, CAPACITY 1,000, WAS SPRING-
TRAINING HOME TO ANY NUMBER OF MINOR-LEAGUE TEAMS.

AH, THE RIGORS OF SPRING TRAINING . . .

would grant you the privilege of holding down the job for McD [the owner of the hotel where the ballplayers stayed] as you did last year.

The other offer, from the Ulysses S. Grant Hotel, San Diego, was sent on April 23, 1913:

I will charge you only $200 per season [at the Grant Hotel] and you can pay me $50 each month on same.

That should make you around $300 for season clear and your monthly [team] payments should make you around $900 for the season and some money this winter if you decide to come with me. . . . Regards to [refreshment] stand. I spoke to you of that. Should make you good money. Dick Souley's wife had the one here and made $70 clear yesterday on cushions, drinks, and cigars. . . .

PLAYERS STAGE A MOCK GAME IN THE OLD FORT IN SAINT AUGUSTINE, FLORIDA, A STOP ON THE SIGHTSEEING LIST OF THE BALLPLAYERS WHO HAD SPRING TRAINING NEARBY.

THE NEWARK BEARS OF THE 1920S DID THE SAME THING BETWEEN GAMES
AS THE PLAYERS OF THE 1990S DO: PLAY CARDS.

Henricks took Edmonton's $810 straight salary, day-off job, and one-way train ticket (we don't know if he won enough games to get train fare home). A year later, letters show, things were going well. Henricks wrote his manager, Deacon White, telling him what a great year 1914 was going to be for him. The week before Christmas 1913 White wrote him the kind of letter every young player dreams of: "Stick to your course and I haven't one shadow of doubt that you will be a sensation next year and go to the big leagues and stick."

. . . .

Henricks was one of thousands of ballplayers in the Canadian minor leagues. Despite the limits on the season due to cold weather that lasts into May, fans in Canada have supported more than twenty minor leagues over the years, although most of those leagues never lasted more than a few seasons. Henricks played in the Western Canada League, with teams in tiny towns like Brandon, Red Deer, and Moose Jaw, and in large cities like Edmonton. It debuted in 1907 and played eight seasons between then and 1921. On the other side of the country, the Eastern Canada League played two seasons in 1928 and 1929, the Cape Breton Colliery League played from 1937 to 1939, and the Quebec Provincial League played the summer of 1940. Most of the Canada leagues were made up of both Canadian teams and American teams from northern states. The Canadian League, playing from 1912 to 1915, had nine teams in Ontario and one in Pennsylvania. The Canadian-American League, playing from 1936 to 1942 and again

from 1946 to 1952, had teams in Ontario, Quebec, New York, and Massachusetts. The Michigan-Ontario League flourished from 1919 to 1925, and the New Brunswick and Maine League played in 1913. Canada also had several teams in the Pacific Coast International League in 1918 and again in the 1920–21 season. A British Columbia team played in the Northwestern League for several years prior to World War I. The Quebec-Ontario-Vermont League played in 1940, and the Provincial League (nine Canadian teams and one American) played from 1950 to 1955. The

AN OPENING-DAY GAME AT NICOLLET PARK IN MINNEAPOLIS.

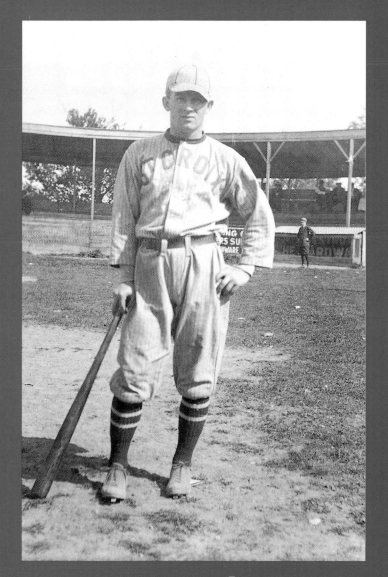
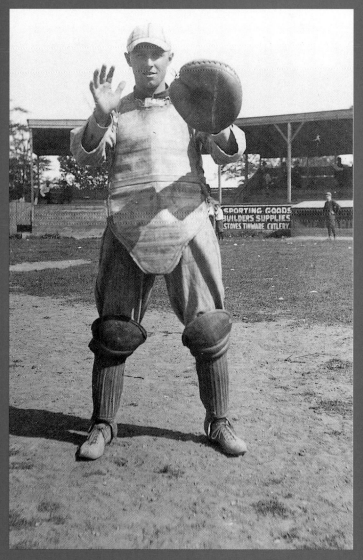

BOTH THESE PLAYERS WERE ON THE ST. CROIX TEAM,
IN CANADA, ABOUT 1910. THESE PHOTOS WERE TAKEN ON
"PICTURE DAY," IN PRESEASON, FOR DISTRIBUTION
TO NEWSPAPERS.

IT WAS WITH HIS BAT, NOT HIS GLOVE, THAT OLVIE CARNEGIE BECAME A MINOR-LEAGUE LEGEND. CARNEGIE HIT 250 HOME RUNS IN HIS CAREER.

Pony League, which played from 1939 to 1956, had teams in Canada, New York, and Pennsylvania.

Most Canadian teams were lower-level, D and C leagues, but Toronto played in the high-level International League as early as 1886, followed by London (Ontario) in 1889. Ottawa joined the league in 1898 and Montreal in 1899. The Montreal team dropped out from 1916 to 1927, but returned in 1928 and built the $1.1 million, eighteen-thousand-seat Montreal Stadium, at the time one of the best in North America. Fans, thirsting for top-level baseball, jammed the ballpark. The Royals flourished and were eventually bought by the major-league Brooklyn Dodgers, who started Jackie Robinson there in 1946 (he later moved up to an outstanding career with the Dodgers), thus sparking the integration of baseball. The Montreal team sagged after the Dodgers sold it in 1958, but remained in the International League until 1960. The Toronto Maple Leafs played in the International League through 1967, building up a large fan base there. That base, plus the core of support for baseball in Montreal, enabled the majors to put franchises in both cities in the 1970s. The zenith of Canadian baseball came in 1992, when the Toronto Blue Jays won the World Series.

In the early 1900s the majors and minors realized they could help each other by booking extensive spring-training tours. Major-league teams would retreat to places like Hot Springs, Arkansas, or Athens, Georgia, practice for three or four weeks, then take a tour through the South, playing four or five games a week against minor-league teams. As early as 1890 the New York Giants were playing annual series against the Galveston (Texas) Sand Crabs. By 1910 most major-league teams were booking full tours in minor-league cities. In one ten-day swing through the South the Giants played in Shreveport, Louisiana; Birmingham, Alabama; Greenville, South Carolina; Greensboro, North Carolina; Norfolk, Virginia; and Waco and Galveston, Texas. That same month, the Brooklyn Dodgers played the Southern League circuit, taking on Memphis, Chattanooga, and Nashville, Tennessee, and Richmond, Virginia. Minor-league teams that were bankrolled by wealthy owners often had their own spring training in southern states and played a steady schedule against local minor-league teams and major-league squads training in the same area.

The minor leagues, like every business, rode the waves of the national economy: in good times people came out to the ballpark; in bad, they did not. The recession that rocked the country in the early 1890s hurt major-league baseball, driving most teams to cut salaries to stay in business. The Spanish-American War of 1898 again affected the majors and crippled many minor-league teams, causing several to go out of business. Competition hurt, too. The majors had been hurt by the Union Association in 1884 and the Players' League in 1890. In 1914 and 1915 they were hurt by another major league, the Federal League, but survived. Operating in larger cities, the Federal League did put several minor-league teams out of business, though. Few of the minor leagues had the cash and resiliency of the majors, which had large markets, experience at marketing (by 1916 the Chicago Cubs had already been in business forty years), wealthy owners, and substantial newspaper coverage and support (New York City had twenty-one daily newspapers in the 1920s).

From 1910 to 1920 there was also intense competition for the entertainment dollar. The majors, in big cities with large populations, could always get their ten thousand or so fans for each game. The new wave of entertainment sweeping the country—silent movies, night clubs, and vaudeville—did not really cut into its gate. In the minors,

where teams drew from a smaller market, a single movie theater with a popular first-run film or an appearance by a touring star like Fannie Brice could cut a game's attendance in half. The movies, lavish city and county fairs, and vaudeville hurt the leagues badly. By 1917 the forty-two leagues in the minors had shrunk to just twenty, and then nearly all were put out of business by the combination of World War I and several events that came on its heels.

The major leagues elected to continue playing baseball through the war, even though many stars enlisted or were drafted. Most minor leagues elected not to play during the war. Many of their players went into the army, and those that stayed home did not want to keep playing a game while the sons of the people in their community were risking their lives overseas. A number of the teams that did not shut down went out of business because, with the government rationing gas and restricting rail travel, they could not draw crowds. When the war ended, just eight minor leagues were able to start up again. A year later the Black Sox scandal, in which eight Chicago White Sox players were accused of fixing the 1919 World Series, rocked the nation. Right on its heels came an equally notorious scandal in the Pacific Coast League, when Salt Lake City's Harl Maggart and Bill Rumler (the league batting champ), San Francisco pitcher Casey Smith, Portland pitcher Tom Seaton (he won twenty-five games that year), and Vernon, California, first baseman Babe Barton were suspended for life for allegedly taking money to throw games. The back-to-back scandals undermined the game of baseball. As the Twenties roared in, the minors were in as much trouble as a nineteen-year-old class D hurler trying to pitch his way out of a jam with the bases loaded in the ninth, two out, darkness falling, and the Terror of Titusville at the plate.

THE BALTIMORE ORIOLES, WHO DROPPED FROM A MAJOR-LEAGUE
CLUB TO A MINOR-LEAGUE ONE IN 1903, BECAME A DYNASTY IN
THE 1920S. THIS IS THE 1923 TEAM, ONE OF SEVEN STRAIGHT
INTERNATIONAL LEAGUE CHAMPIONS.

CHAPTER THREE

IN FULL SWING

The fans began to congregate along the sidewalks of Greenmount Avenue in Baltimore late in the morning on a mild April day in 1922. They wanted to get a good view of the long parade that always marked opening day for the Orioles, the undisputed champions of the International League. Ice-cream and soda vendors worked the crowds. Women gently rocked baby carriages back and forth. Men took off their straw boaters from time to time to straighten their slicked-back hair. Thousands of kids, playing hooky from school (nobody really minded because, after all, it was opening day), ran through the crowd, jockeying for positions where they could get autographs when the open cars drove by. At the gates to the park newsboys with incredibly loud sing-song voices hawked special opening-day editions of the news-papers. Inside the park the stands filled up quickly to their capacity of sixteen thousand as the parade began several miles away. Jack Dunn, the savior of minor-league baseball in Baltimore and the owner-manager of the team, was in the lead car. Behind him, in a dozen cars, were the players of the greatest minor-league dynasty of the 1920s.

The Orioles were unique in America in April of 1922. They were a minor-league team that had been, just a gen-eration before, the best major-league team in the country,

winning three straight national-league pennants in 1894, 1895, and 1896, with a superstar lineup that included five future Hall of Famers. The O's joined the majors with the American Association in 1882, went into the National League when the association folded, and in 1898 were torn apart in an internal power play. The owner, Gerald Van Der Horst, convinced he could make more money in New York than in Baltimore, bought a large interest in the Brooklyn club, transferred manager Ned Hanlon and sev-eral Baltimore stars there, and let the Orioles drown. In 1900 the National League shrunk from twelve to eight clubs and booted out the weakened O's. The Orioles crawled back into the majors as an American League team in 1901, but the city's franchise in the league was transferred to New York in 1903 in yet another political donnybrook (there, it became the Yankees).

Manager Hanlon felt bad about the mess he helped create and in 1903, with his own money, bought a minor-league franchise and moved it to Baltimore. The Orioles were reborn as a member of the Eastern League. The eccentric Jack Dunn became manager in 1907. He took the Orioles to a pennant in 1908 and bought the team outright from Hanlon in 1910. He signed a kid named Babe Ruth, from a local orphanage, in 1914, in a decade that saw him ink some of the best young players in the game. Nobody ever figured out how he found so many good ones. In that first year on the team, Ruth hit a ball off the right-field wall so hard that the line-drive ricochet was caught by the second baseman.

Getting players was easy, but keeping the Orioles in business was not. No sooner did Dunn sign Ruth, who was immediately, at nineteen, the best pitcher in the International League (the old Eastern took that name in 1911), than the Federal League landed in Baltimore in 1914 with a brand-new ballpark. The Federals, a third major league,

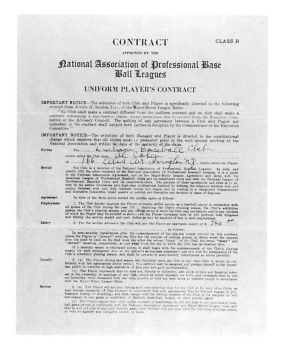

ALTA COHEN SIGNED THIS DURHAM BULLS CONTRACT IN 1929, AGREEING TO PLAY A SIX-MONTH SEASON AT $200 A MONTH.

ALTA COHEN, ROCKY MOUNT, NORTH CAROLINA, 1929.

swamped the Orioles at the gate. Dunn's business was so bad that by midsummer he was almost bankrupt. To keep the team he had to sell off half a dozen players to the majors, including Ruth, whom he genuinely liked (the Babe went for all of $2,800 to the Red Sox). These sales didn't save Dunn, however. In 1915 he left town, taking the Orioles to Richmond to play in the Virginia League, where he also lost money. Fortunately for Dunn and the O's, the Federal League folded after the 1915 season. The Orioles moved back to Baltimore and managed to get the new Federal League ballpark, now vacant, as a home. Stable at last, Dunn began to build his dynasty. Fans, who saw the Federal League as their very last chance at the majors, embraced the minor-league Orioles and, almost overnight,

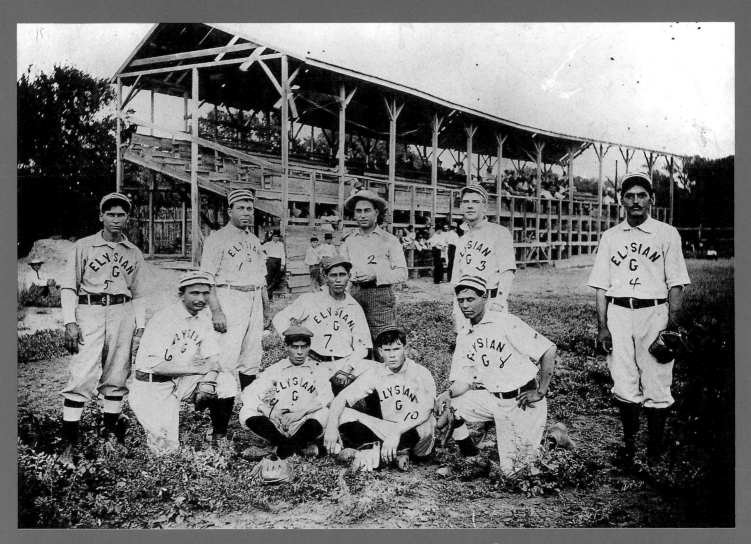

RICKETY GRANDSTANDS WERE STANDARD IN SMALL SOUTHWEST
BALLPARKS AT THE TURN OF THE CENTURY. THE ELYSIAN FIELDS
TEAM FROM ARIZONA POSED IN FRONT OF THIS OLD WOODEN ONE.

Baltimore became one of the most devoted minor-league cities in America.

Fans remember Orioles Park, where the team resided longest, until the 1940s, as the best of their stadiums. "The seats were very close to the field, so you'd practically be part of the game," says Mike Kawecki, who was a fan there in the 1930s. "So close you could hear what the first baseman said to the pitcher."

Baltimore's Dunn had some of the best players in baseball in the 1920s, including Joe Boley, Fritz Maisel, John Honig, Socks Seibold, George Earnshaw, and Jack Ogden (he pitched thirty-one winning games in 1921), and Max Bishop, who played well for several years in Baltimore before he was sold to the Philadelphia A's, where he had a fine career, hitting .271. Dunn had superstar Jack Bentley, a pitcher who posted a 41–5 record in three seasons on the mound and hit over .330 every year, topping out with a sensational .412 average in 1921 (he was later sold to the New

EVERYBODY WAS PUMPED UP FOR THIS TEAM PICTURE OF A 1909 TUCSON MINOR-LEAGUE CLUB. NOTE THE GRAND POSTURES OF THE CATCHER (SECOND FROM LEFT) AND PITCHER (SECOND FROM RIGHT, BACK ROW).

York Giants). And he had the great Lefty Grove, a legendary pitcher who in four and a half years with the Orioles won 108 games and lost just 36. Grove was the minor league's strikeout king, fanning 330 in the summer of 1923 and 1,118 in four seasons. He went on to a Hall of Fame career in the majors.

With good players and strong fan and city support the Orioles won the International League pennant in 1919. That year they won a startling 100 games and lost 49. It was the beginning of the greatest single championship run in the history of professional baseball. In 1920 the O's won the International League flag again, this time taking 109 games. In 1921 they won a record 119 games to take their third straight pennant. They were invincible, winning pennants again in 1922, 1923, 1924, and 1925. When the run was over, the Orioles had taken seven straight pennants, winning an average of 111 games a year. In 1923 they beat the Yankees, who won the World Series that year, in an exhibition game.

The Orioles were not the only powerhouse of the 1920s. On the West Coast the San Francisco Seals won the Pacific Coast League title five times in a ten-year stretch, winning 138 games in 1925 with superstars like future major leaguers Willie Kamm and Paul Waner. Up North the Rochester, New York, Red Wings won pennants in the International League in 1928, 1929, 1930, and 1931. In the Midwest, Saint Paul won four titles in six years (1919 to 1924) in the American Association. Fort Worth won seven straight Texas League titles, beginning in 1919. New Orleans won the Southern League championship four times between 1926 and 1934. The super teams pumped up attendance at home and doubled and tripled attendance wherever they played on the road. Their success encouraged entrepreneurs to start up some of the defunct leagues again and to begin new leagues,

and by the middle of the 1920s the eight minor leagues had grown to twenty-five.

Minor-league baseball came to the Southwest in the early days of the century, and its arrival was as wild as that of cowboys coming into town on a Saturday night at the end of a long cattle drive. Minor-league ball had been played in Texas since the late 1880s, and over the years minor leagues had come and gone in Kansas, Nebraska, and Colorado. It wasn't until the 1920s, though, that baseball bloomed in the deserts and the turbulent mining towns of Arizona, Nevada, and New Mexico. And, just as in the frontier days of old, the atmosphere of baseball in the Southwest was rough and tumble, in many areas involving teams from Mexico, just across the border. (One Mexican stadium was so close to the border that home runs were literally hit out of the country.)

Arizona ballparks in the 1920s were in hot, arid desert and had no grass. Games were played on the hard dirt, and fielders took their lives in their hands on bad bounces. Team sponsors, with hardly enough money for player salaries, spent little on the stadiums. Most were just one-thousand- to two-thousand-seat stadiums with bleacher seating wrapped around home plate. Many had no roofs, and fans baked in the hot desert sun.

Typical of the rugged baseball played in the Southwest was the May 29, 1921, battle between the White Sox of Douglas, Arizona, and their arch rivals, the Nogales Crows of Sonora, Mexico. Thousands of fans from both teams (two of the best in the Southwest) showed up, and the game had to be moved to a ten-thousand-seat stadium in Mexico, which quickly filled with twenty-thousand spectators. Armed Mexican soldiers surrounded the field because rumors were rife that Mexican revolutionary Pancho Villa might attack the stadium. The hotly contested game was scoreless in the ninth when Tachi Ruiz, of Douglas, hit a triple. He slid into third, knocking the base fifteen feet away. The Nogales fielder, seeing Ruiz sitting on the site of third, and the bag near the stands, tagged him. The umpire called Ruiz out and hundreds of Douglas fans, screaming "Fix!" poured onto the field, starting a riot. The governor of Sonora ordered the soldiers to clear the field. A soldier, knocked down by the crowds, accidentally fired his rifle in the air. Panic struck. The soldiers opened fire on the crowd, killing one and wounding twelve. The dead and wounded were carted off the field and—this could happen only in the Wild West—the game resumed, almost as if nothing had happened. Nogales won.

The Southwest was a seemingly endless well of outrageous activity. It had been a magnet for desperadoes in the frontier days and in the 1920s attracted baseball's desperadoes—namely the Black Sox of Chicago, the eight players who had been kicked out of baseball for life for fixing the 1919 World Series. The commissioner of baseball, Kenesaw Mountain Landis, had ruled they could not play in any major or minor league. The hundreds of minor-league teams across the country would not touch the banned players for fear of Landis's wrath, but in the Wild West people didn't fear gunslingers and bank robbers, much less Judge Landis.

In 1925 towns in Arizona, New Mexico, and Mexico formed the Frontier League. The Douglas, Arizona, team was led by "Prince" Hal Chase, who had been playing on semipro teams in Arizona for three years. Chase had been informally booted out of baseball in 1920 over numerous allegations that he had been betting on games when he played with the New York Giants. When the 1925 season started he was named player-manager of the Douglas Blues

and told to hire whomever he wanted—and to win. That first season he brought in two of the Black Sox, Chick Gandhil and Buck Weaver, and tried to get two other outlawed players, pitching ace Eddie Cicotte (he won twenty-nine games in 1919) and Shoeless Joe Jackson (he demanded $500 a week)—but failed. Another banned player, Jimmie O'Connell, reported to have "influenced" games when he played with the Giants, also joined the league. In 1926, when the league changed its name to the Copper League, another outlawed Black Sox star, pitcher Lefty Williams, joined Douglas. Right on his heels came the mysterious Roy Counts, who simply arrived and asked for a tryout. He was signed and played well but left the team suddenly one day when it was discovered he was an escaped convict from an Oklahoma prison.

Dwight Patterson, now 92, played against Chase in 1922 in an Arizona semipro league. He remembers: "We didn't pay much attention to Judge Landis. Arizona was out in the middle of nowhere, with just one or two train lines connecting us to the world. Who cared about banned ballplayers? We just wanted good ballplayers and those guys were terrific. Hal Chase was a good hitter, but he was one of the best fielders you ever saw—as good as anybody you see today. Buck Weaver was a great hitter. Hit everything. Pitchers couldn't fool him. Williams was a terrific pitcher. You could see right away what great ballplayers they must have been in Chicago."

Weaver and Gandhil did not arrive in Arizona until mid-season in 1925, when the Douglas nine was mired in the cellar, but the two superstars were enough to shoot last-place Douglas into first. They lost the pennant over a scheduling controversy, however (after which Gandhil temporarily left the team to make playoff money with one of the other

A 1905 photo of primitive minor-league baseball in the Southwest. The umpire stands behind the pitcher to call balls and strikes, the infield is all dirt, and the outfield fence is a low hedge of some kind. The players are using half a bench as a dugout; their fans occupy the other half.

teams in the league). Nonetheless, the outlawed major leaguers had banner years in the desert: O'Connell hit .558 in 1926; Gandhil and Weaver were consistently hitting .300 and often pitched, too.

After the Black Sox scandal Lefty Williams had pitched on semipro teams in the Chicago area in 1921 and 1922 but began to drink. On the Douglas team he was a good pitcher when sober, and impossible to get a hit off of when he had some "soda," as he referred to his refreshments. The southpaw kept a bottle in the dugout and

would take a nip between innings. The local press reported that he pitched well in the first half of each game and brilliantly in the second half. Once, having misread his pitching schedule, he was found drunk in a local bar right before a game. With no time to dry out, and no other pitcher ready, he was put on the mound anyway and pitched one of the greatest games of his career.

Far from the deserts of Arizona, a Minnesota team called the Scobey Touring Pros, a semipro club formed by wealthy miners that traveled throughout the north country,

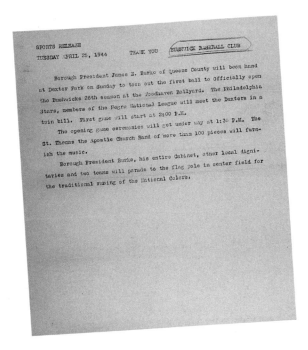

THE BUSHWICKS WERE A NEW YORK CITY INDEPENDENT TEAM OF TRIPLE A STATURE WHO PLAYED A SCHEDULE OF INDEPENDENT CLUBS AND A NUMBER OF TRAVELING NEGRO LEAGUE TEAMS.

was beating just about everybody. The reason? Like their brethren in the Southwest, the miners went out and hired two of the Black Soxers—Hap Felsch and Swede Risberg. The two sluggers, each hitting over .400, led the team to a sensational season, taking on all comers and beating some local minor-league teams, too.

Another phenomenon that baseball saw in the 1920s was the flourishing of the Negro Leagues. Ever since baseball had been segregated at the end of the nineteenth century, good black players had been playing on all-black teams. As with the white teams, these teams took all forms: Some stayed in their home cities and played other black teams, others barnstormed through their regions, playing other black teams, and the best barnstormed through the country, playing black and white teams wherever they could find them. From 1890 to 1920 barnstorming black teams, such as the Lincoln Giants (New York) and the Chicago Giants, played more than a hundred games against the New York Yankees, the New York Giants, the Detroit Tigers, the Philadelphia A's, and other major-league teams. The black teams won half these games (a black team defeated the Philadelphia Phillies the week after they won the National League pennant), giving urgency to demands that baseball be integrated. But the powers that be weren't going to allow that to happen, so in 1920 the Negro National League was formed, with teams in Detroit; Indianapolis; Kansas City, Kansas; Cincinnati; Chicago; Saint Louis; and Columbus, Ohio. The Eastern Colored League formed in 1923 and a third black league, the Negro Association League, was born in 1929. These teams played each other half the year and barnstormed the other half, taking on as many minor-league teams, black or white, as they could to make money. The black Kansas City Monarchs beat the white minor-league Kansas City Blues, with whom they shared a stadium, in the highest-attendance game in Kansas City history in 1922. These games meant more publicity and revenue for the minor-league clubs who took on the barnstorming black superstars.

The Negro National League and, later, the Negro American League, were true major leagues. Employing the best black players (and thus some of the country's best players period), they played in large cities, drew crowds of twenty thousand and more, and went head to head with the white major leagues. The success of the Negro Leagues spurred local entrepreneurs to sponsor black teams and black leagues. Black teams managed to stay in business for much of the 1920s and 1930s, thrilling crowds in small towns and big cities across the nation. One thing that pulled in the crowds was the opportunity to see a big-league star, and black minor-league teams ballyhooed any big-league black stars they were able to sign up for the season. In 1939 the touring Washington-Philadelphia Pilots sent out hundreds of advertising broadsides with a huge photo of their star attraction, Darius "Buzz" Bea, formerly a pitcher with the Philadelphia Stars and Baltimore Elite Giants of the larger Negro National League.

New York City had a black minor league with eight teams, including the Hellfighters, made up of black World War I vets. Washington, D.C., with a population that was 35 percent black, had a popular league with such teams as the Washington Athletics, YMCA, Alcores, Guild, and Naval Reserve. In Cincinnati black entrepreneur Tom Ellis headed a black minor league that drew big enough crowds to lease the Reds' ballpark. Teams there included the Pekin Specials, Eighth Ward Stars, East End Hawks, Emeralds, Zenias, Thunderbirds, and the wondrously named White City Bear Cats.

Black minor-league teams in Texas formed a highly organized, state-wide black circuit, the Texas Negro League, with teams in San Antonio, Austin, Galveston, and other cities. They often leased white minor-league parks for games, but white teams in Texas, a state bordering on the Deep South, were reluctant to play the black minor-league teams. The teams of the Texas Negro League found plenty of challenge, however, battling one another and picking up hundreds of games with professional teams in bordering Mexico, where there was no segregation.

There were black minor-league teams in many other cities as well, large and small alike. Some of the best teams were the Muncie (Indiana) Cubs, the Montgomery (Ala-

bama) Grey Sox, the New Orleans Black Eagles, the Pennsylvania Colored Giants, the Memphis Tigers, the Sumter (South Carolina) Gamecocks, the Kokomo (Indiana) Red Sox, and the Evansville (Indiana) Colored Braves. The black minors tended to play most of their games outside their league. They played a league schedule of just thirty or

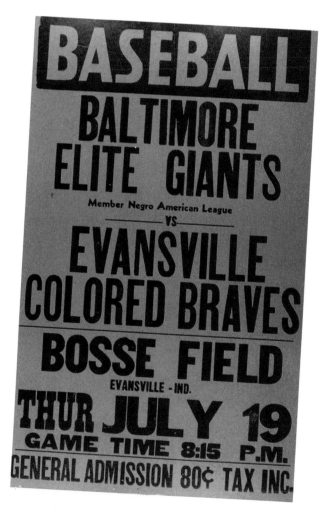

BEFORE BASEBALL WAS INTEGRATED, BLACK PROFESSIONAL TEAMS LEASED LOCAL MINOR-LEAGUE PARKS TO PLAY OTHER BLACK TEAMS.

THE KANSAS CITY MONARCHS WERE ONE OF THE TOP
NEGRO LEAGUE TEAMS THAT BARNSTORMED THE COUNTRY
PLAYING LOCAL MINOR-LEAGUE TEAMS.

league team of the 1930s, toured throughout New Jersey. Several busloads of fans followed the team to away games, and fans and players would get together before or after the games for picnics. The Mohawk Giants, of Schenectady, New York, were an exception, traveling the country on a two-hundred-game schedule year after year.

How good was the level of baseball played in the black minors? "Very competitive," says Ernie Banks, who played with the Amarillo (Texas) Colts in the late 1940s and then with the Kansas City Monarchs before moving directly to the Chicago Cubs and becoming a superstar. "They were out to beat you and beat you bad. The pitching was good, the hitting was good, the runners fast. It was good, hard baseball. I don't think, looking back, I could have had better training for the majors than playing in the black minors. The players I faced were just as good as the players in the white minors."

so games and then toured the rest of the time, adding another sixty or seventy games. (White minor-league teams, by contrast, played each other in a schedule of a hundred or so games, then added another ten or twelve exhibitions against a major-league club, barnstorming all-star team, or a black-league team.) Even when touring, black minors usually stuck to their regions, though, and did little long-distance traveling. The Madison Colored Giants, of Madison, Wisconsin, for example, played a short home schedule and then traveled throughout the state, playing other black teams and many white semipro teams. The Montclair (New Jersey) Giants, a black minor-

IN THE 1920S, AS NOW, PLAYERS PAID CAREFUL
ATTENTION TO WHAT THE PRESS SAID ABOUT THEM.

SPORTSWRITERS WERE A DAPPER GROUP IN THE ROARING TWENTIES.
SNAPPILY DRESSED SPORTS COLUMNIST FRANK FAGAN (RIGHT) INTERVIEWS
HOWARD FREEMAN OF THE NEWARK BEARS IN 1928.

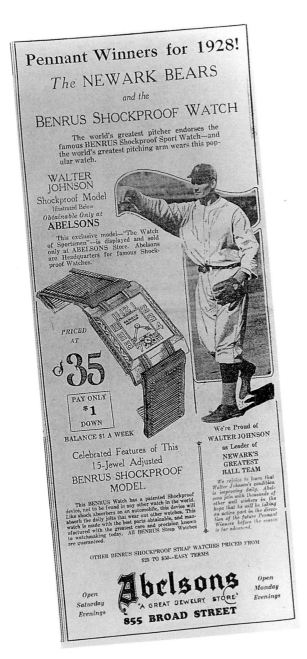

UNTIL THE 1950S, JUST ABOUT EVERY SUNDAY NEWSPAPER IN AMERICA CARRIED *BOYS' WORLD*, A SUPPLEMENT THAT OFTEN FEATURED ARTICLES ON MINOR-LEAGUE BASEBALL WITH SIMPLISTIC LIFE LESSONS THROWN IN.

STAR PLAYERS OR MANAGERS ON MINOR-LEAGUE TEAMS OFTEN LANDED LUCRATIVE ADVERTISING CONTRACTS IN THEIR TOWNS. WALTER JOHNSON HAWKED ABELSONS JEWELRY IN NEWARK.

The black minors played the same roles in their communities that the white minor-league teams did in theirs: They provided athletic entertainment for the black community and they gave youngsters the opportunity to be ballplayers. But in the highly segregated society of America in the 1920s, they had an additional function, shared with black churches, schools, night clubs, and theaters: They built the foundation for a separate black culture that fostered heritage, pride, and opportunity.

As the 1920s unfolded, the game of baseball changed. Technological advances sweeping the country after World War I had two effects: They brought the game to a wider audience, with improvements to printing technology and transportation; and they altered the pace and action of the game itself, with the development of a new type of ball.

Armed with improved printing capabilities, newspapers could reproduce photographs beautifully. Editors liked two types of pictures—those of baseball players and those of movie stars—and they stuffed their newspapers with both. The pictures of local stars in minor-league cities all over the United States helped build a whole new fan base. Innovative photography, action pictures, and fine reproduction made sports as much a part of the oft-read family newspapers as local news and the comics.

By the middle of the 1920s just about every small city in the United States had some kind of mass transit. Streetcar lines ran throughout town, making it easy for fans to get to and from the ballpark, and most trips cost just a nickel. By the 1920s millions of Americans had automobiles, mass-produced and available for $600, sometimes less. People in minor-league cities and towns, and, importantly, those living ten or fifteen miles away, could now get to the ballpark in minutes. Minor-league teams managed to hold ticket prices down to just twenty-five or fifty cents, increasing their appeal.

A big change came to the game itself when, beginning in 1920, the "lively ball"—a more tightly wound baseball that went much farther when hit—came into use. High-scoring games, with .300-plus batting averages and lots of hits, made the minors a carnival of scoring, to the delight of fans. Many players hit over .400 in a season (Ike Boone hit .448 in the Pacific Coast League in 1930), and several tallied more than two hundred RBIs. In 1924 Lyman Lamb of Tulsa hit one hundred doubles. A player named Paul Strand, of Salt Lake City, had 325 hits in 1923. And a proliferation of home runs—a product of the "lively ball"—developed new interest in the minor-league game. Babe Ruth slammed fifty-four homers in 1920, the year he was traded to the New York Yankees. In a single season the slugger helped create a boom for a generation. Minor-league cities featured older and smaller ballparks, some with fences just 240 or 250 feet away from home plate. In these small fields the lively ball, allow-

ing entire teams to hit over .300, ushered in a new generation of home-run hitters. Tony Lazzeri hit sixty home runs in Salt Lake City in 1925, two years before Ruth did it in New York, and drove in 222 runs. Ike Boone hit fifty-five homers in the Pacific Coast League in 1929; Big Joe Hauser hit sixty-three for Baltimore in 1930 and sixty-nine for Minneapolis in 1933; and Buzz Arlett hit fifty-four for Baltimore in 1932. Nick Cullop hit fifty-four for Minneapolis in

SCORECARDS, SUCH AS THIS ONE FROM 1936, WERE CHOCK-FULL OF ENTICING ADS.

A SINGLE-TIER GRANDSTAND WITH A WOODEN ROOF HELD UP BY PILLARS WAS THE
STANDARD 1920S MINOR-LEAGUE BALLPARK.

NICOLLET PARK, IN MINNEAPOLIS, WAS AN ALL-WOOD PARK WITH AN ALL-WOOD
DUGOUT. THE MILLERS ARE PACKED INTO THIS ONE, WHOSE ONLY AMENITY IS A
BRAND-NEW WATER COOLER (FAR LEFT). NOTE HOW WELL THE FANS ARE DRESSED.

IN THE 1920S FANS OFTEN EXITED THE BALLPARK BY WALKING DOWN TO THE
FIELD AND THEN OUT LARGE OPEN GATES.

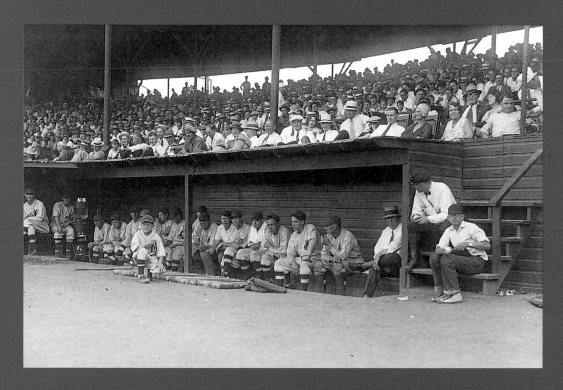

had stadiums that seated more than forty thousand spectators because they could draw that many to a game. Minor-league teams drew only about five to six thousand fans, so they built small, one-level ballparks to accommodate those numbers. The small parks lent an air of intimacy to the game, drawing fans much closer to their teams. Such institutions as Ladies' Day, a prominent fixture on minor-league schedules by the 1920s, and, later in the decade, "Knot Hole Gangs," discount-ticket clubs for kids, further stoked fan loyalty.

The pageantry surrounding minor-league ball in many towns was a reflection of those close ties between team and

EMMA SEARS WITH HER FATHER (RIGHT) AND BIG BROTHER BILL, MINOR-LEAGUE HURLER AND THE LOCAL HERO OF TINY BUTLER, NEW JERSEY, IN 1927.

1930 and went on to hit 420 lifetime; Moose Clabaugh hit sixty-two for Tyler, in the East Texas League, in 1926, and 346 lifetime. Bunny Brief, another 1920s star who gained fame with both Kansas City and Milwaukee, totaled 342; Spencer Harris, who debuted in 1921 and played for twenty-seven years, hit 258 in all.

Even though minor-league baseball was reaching more and more people, the teams still retained their close ties to their communities. Most major-league teams in the 1920s

THESE WOMEN ARRIVED AT THE BALLPARK EARLY AND GRABBED FIRST-ROW SEATS. LADIES' DAY, STARTED IN THE 1880S, WAS ONE OF THE MOST POPULAR PROMOTIONS IN THE MINORS.

A TRADITION ON OPENING DAY WAS FOR A BAND TO LEAD BOTH TEAMS IN A
PARADE ACROSS THE PLAYING FIELD.

community. Major-league teams, of course, had parades when they returned from a World Series, but the minors were applauded by their communities throughout the season. They started with parades on opening day, followed by picnics, speakers, and festivities. On the Fourth of July and other holidays there was always some sort of celebration at the local minor-league ballpark. All season long, ball games, particularly Sunday doubleheaders, were the center of small-town community life. People came by the thousands to picnic near the park before the game. Afterwards, local bands gave concerts on the field, and fans remained to listen as cool breezes drifted across the ballpark. Sometimes dances were held right on the field. And at least once

a year every minor-league team worth its logo brought in a major-league team for an exhibition game, at which the big-league heros were paraded around the field to the cheers of the crowd.

Local newspapers joined in the festivities by sponsoring "most popular player" contests. The Newark Bears in the 1930s kept week-by-week vote tallies, as fans cast ballots for their favorite player, who was crowned at a game at the end of the season and showered with gifts. Major leaguers who had played in a minor-league town, or had grown up there, often were brought back for a day in their honor at the town's ballpark to pump up ticket sales; a dinner usually followed. Ballplayers who fancied themselves

THE ANNUAL OPENING DAY PARADE IN SACRAMENTO USED TO FEATURE THE SACRAMENTO
AND OAKLAND PLAYERS RIDING IN OPEN CARS BEHIND BRASS BANDS DOWN THE MAIN STREETS AS
TENS OF THOUSANDS CHEERED.

singers sometimes performed on local radio shows, their appearance helping, of course, to sell tickets. In one of the wildest stretches of ballplayer entertainment, the Macon (Georgia) Peaches staged a variety show to raise money for a 1928 post-season tour of South America. A quartet of infielders sang "Everything Is Peaches Down in Georgia," a pitcher who nicknamed himself Caruso sang "Where the River Shannon Flows," two outfielders did a soft shoe, and two others imitated radio personalities Amos & Andy. Future pitching star Dazzy Vance and Happy Harry Snyder dressed up as Frank and Jesse James for a Wild West number, with two league umpires playing bank robbers.

A roster of the gimmicks and stunts performed over the years in the interest of generating enthusiasm (and sales) for the game of baseball might go on forever. In 1890 a skydiver jumped out of a hot-air balloon into a Los Angeles ballpark. A biplane flew low over another Los Angeles park on an opening day in the early 1920s as the pilot dropped a ball over home plate. As the ball hurtled to earth, the town's mayor tried to hit it with a bat and failed, eliciting sustained boos from the delighted crowd. As early as 1894 a midget named Tom Michaels was hiring himself out as an attraction to dozens of minor-league teams each summer. A midget named Eddie Gaedel batted (just once) for Saint Louis in the 1940s.

But what the fans of the minor leagues really came to see were the players. Most teams put the same roster on the field year after year, and that basic playing unit represented the town, be it Waterloo, Iowa; Tucson, Arizona; or Sacramento, California. The team formed a strong bond (to a degree rarely found in the majors) with the fans. It was a family and like a family it stayed together. The fans did not come out to see individual superstars, or even a winning team; they came to see "their boys." The bonds grew so strong that managers and owners were reluctant to trade or sell stars to other teams, and talented players who were just not good enough for the majors found they could play in a minor-league city for close to ten or more years. Among those with staying power over the years were Pep Clark, with Milwaukee for twelve straight years, 1904 to 1916, hitting .290; Danny Boone, who played seven straight years with Saint Paul in the 1920s; George Detore, on the San Diego team in the Pacific Coast League for eight straight

years in the 1930s; Andrew Reese, nine straight years with Memphis, 1931 to 1939; and Wayne Blackburn, who played six straight seasons for Indianapolis in the 1940s.

Because it was possible to sustain a long career in the minors, forty-year-old players were common in the leagues. Hundreds of players who would have been washed up in the majors at thirty-five found that they could extend

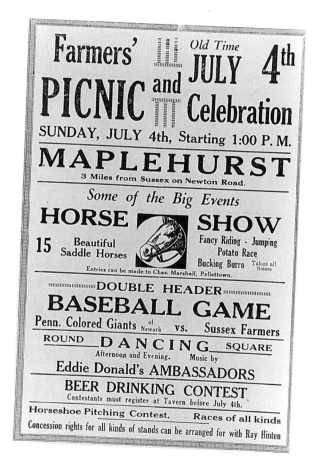

MINOR-LEAGUE GAMES WERE THE LINCHPIN OF FOURTH OF JULY CELEBRATIONS IN THE 1930S. A SINGLE COUNTY MIGHT HAVE AS MANY AS TWENTY DOUBLEHEADERS ON THAT ONE DAY, SANDWICHED BETWEEN PICNICS, HORSE SHOWS, DANCES, AND BEER-DRINKING CONTESTS.

Firestone
MARK OF QUALITY
Means
First Class
RUBBER HEELS
distributed by
Bolduc & Bolduc
123-125 Middle St.
Portland, Me.

NEWSPAPERS IN SMALL TOWNS AND CITIES WOULD GIVE AS MUCH PROMINENCE TO MINOR-LEAGUE BOX SCORES, LIKE THESE OF THE NEW ENGLAND LEAGUE, AS MAJOR CITIES WOULD GIVE THE YANKEES OR CUBS.

him a spot in the Hall of Fame. The Iron Man came to the minors in 1909 to pitch for Newark and hurled 422 innings that year for a 29–16 record, with eleven shutouts. Always reliable (he called his bread-and-butter sidearm curve ball "Old Sal"), he won thirty games the following year and, through the 1925 season, won a total of 207 games, giving him a combined major/minor record of 482–357, exceeded only by Cy Young's 511 wins. (So many pitchers toiled in the minors for decades that twelve tallied more than 200 wins.) In his final year in Dubuque, when he was fifty-four,

their careers by ten years or more in the minors, where their skills were still appreciated. Iron Man Joe McGinnity, who left the major leagues at the age of thirty-seven, successfully pitched in the minors until he was fifty-four, often pitching both ends of a doubleheader. As a former big-league star who could be counted on to take the mound year after year, McGinnity became an even bigger star and gate attraction in the minors than he had been with the New York Giants. His records in the minors were just as impressive as his records in the majors, which had earned

EXERCISE . . . EXERCISE . . . EXERCISE . . .

JACK FOURNIER PLAYED WITH THE CHICAGO WHITE SOX
IN 1912 AND THEN WITH THE YANKEES, THE SAINT LOUIS
BROWNS, THE BROOKLYN DODGERS, AND THE BOSTON
BRAVES. IN 1928, AT AGE THIRTY-SEVEN, HE BEGAN AN
EXTENDED MINOR-LEAGUE CAREER IN NEWARK, NEW JERSEY.

BIG LUKE EASTER PLAYED FOR THE CLEVELAND INDIANS.
THEN, WHEN HIS MAJOR-LEAGUE DAYS WERE OVER, HE
CONTINUED TO PLAY INTO HIS FORTIES FOR THE BUFFALO
BISONS. HE LATER WENT TO WORK FOR A BANK AND
WAS KILLED IN A HOLDUP.

LARRY BARTON WAS ONE OF MANY WHO PLAYED INTO HIS
FORTIES. BARTON PLAYED ON TWENTY DIFFERENT TEAMS IN
A TWENTY-FOUR-YEAR CAREER.

A SHUTTERBUG COULD BE FOUND ON EVERY TEAM,
TAKING PICTURES TO MAIL HOME.

McGinnity faced, and beat, an eighteen-year-old pitcher born the year he retired from the majors.

Double Duty Radcliffe, a black star, played until he was fifty-four on different Canadian minor-league teams. Edward "Old Folks" Pilette hurled in the Pacific Coast League for twenty-eight years, retiring at forty-eight. In

1949 Orie Arntzen, age forty, posted a 25–2 record with Albany and was named player of the year in the minors by the *Sporting News*. He pitched for twenty-three years, twenty-two of them in the minors. Myril Hoag, a decent major-league outfielder for ten years, retrained himself as a pitcher and extended his career in the minors by seven years, striking out 280 batters for Gainesville, Florida, in 1949 when he was forty-one. Wes Ferrell, a notable major-league pitcher who won 193 games in his career and had six 20-win seasons, retooled himself as an outfielder when his pitching days were over and played six more years in the minors, hitting .349, finally retiring at forty-two. Jim O'Rourke, a major leaguer in the 1890s with the Giants, was still catching in the minors at age sixty. Walter "Boom Boom" Beck, a disaster in the majors, managed to pitch in the minors until he was forty-six, winning 199 games in the 1930s and 1940s. In 1980 Hub Kittle, another veteran of twenty-plus years, appeared in his last game as a pitcher—he was sixty-three.

Hall of Famer Ray Dandridge, a Negro National League star who went to the majors when the color line was broken in 1947, pitched in the minors until he was forty-two. Luke Easter's last at bat for the Rochester (New York) Red Wings was at the age of forty-nine. Fred "Pap" Williams led the Alabama-Florida league in stolen bases (forty-four) in 1954, when he was forty-one. Luke "Hot Potato" Hamlin, who spent five years with the Dodgers in mid-career and won twenty for them in 1939, pitched in the minors for twenty-two years, finishing the 1947 season in Toronto with a 15–6 record and leading the league in ERAs with a 2.22—at age forty-one. He pitched his last game at age forty-four. Nick Cullop played in the minors for twenty-five years, and Slugger Joe Hauser played until he was forty-three.

The minors also gave young players chances they never would have had in the majors. Small-town clubs took on teenagers, reasoning that they had a good prospect if the player was decent and had lost nothing if he was not. Players were supposed to be at least eighteen, but kids often lied about their age, going into the minors at sixteen or seventeen. Most youngsters worked cheap, too, and the small-town teams had tight budgets to worry about. The fans enjoyed seeing local boys on the team; they could judge for themselves how good the town's high school hotshot was. Some were pretty good. On July 26, 1889, Willie McGill, age fifteen, pitched a 3–0 no-hitter for Evansville, Indiana, over Davenport, Iowa, in the Central Inter-State League.

In a July 19, 1952, game in the Georgia State League the Fitzgerald team was being hammered 13–0, when fans began to howl, "Put in the batboy!" Why not? thought the manager. The lad could do no worse than the players. So in the eighth inning he put twelve-year-old batboy Joe Relford into the game in center field, where he made a spectacular catch (though he grounded out at the plate). Jimmy Reese, who went on to play with the Yankees, was

OUT IN ARIZONA IN THE 1920S, WE PLAYED MOST OF OUR GAMES IN THE MINING CAMPS UP NORTH. THE DIAMOND AND OUTFIELD WERE HARD DIRT AND FULL OF SNAKES. IN THE TINY CLUBHOUSES, THERE WOULD BE ONE SHOWER NOZZLE FOR THE WHOLE TEAM AND NO LOCKERS, JUST HOOKS ON THE WALL AND A SINGLE OLD BENCH. MOST OF THE FANS, OFTEN AS MANY AS A THOUSAND, JUST STOOD ALONG THE SIDELINES. IF YOU PLAYED OUTFIELD YOU HAD TO WATCH OUT BECAUSE BY THE SEVENTH INNING SOME FANS HAD TOO MUCH LIQUOR TO DRINK AND THEY'D WALK INTO THE OUTFIELD AND WANDER AROUND.

—DWIGHT PATTERSON, OF PHOENIX

THIS BALLPLAYER AND TWO FRIENDS ARE AT AN INDOOR POOL IN ONE
OF COLUMBIA, SOUTH CAROLINA'S MOST LUXURIOUS HOTELS, 1928.

stuck into a Pacific Coast League game when he was four-teen and played several innings. Otto McIver, thirteen, played outfield for the San Antonio Broncos in 1908, and Frank Kitchens, also thirteen, was the catcher for the Houston Buffaloes that same year. When the Pacific Coast League's Los Angeles team was short on players because of World War II, they signed a fifteen-year-old high school

sophomore as a catcher and got him into dozens of games. He often caught with pitcher Charlie Root, then forty-four years old, making them the oldest and youngest battery ever to play together. The youngest player ever was George Diggins, just nine. He was the Concord, New Hampshire, team mascot on June 25, 1904, in a game against Lowell, Massachusetts, in the New England League. Concord had only ten players in all. One left the game injured and another was thrown out, leaving eight. Diggins volunteered to play, nobody objected, and the nine-year-old went in for three innings and batted once (struck out).

Another draw for fans was the presence of brothers on a team. There have been some brothers who played together on major-league teams (Walker and Morton Cooper of the Saint Louis Cardinals, for instance), but brother combinations have been common in minor-league ball through the years. Minor-league teams and state leagues happily signed local brothers because they were always good gate attractions, sparking fan loyalty. Hundreds of locals would come out to see how the Jones brothers, town heroes all those years through grade school and high school, would do against professionals. There were hundreds of brother combinations in the minors. The Dean brothers, Dizzy and Daffy, both pitched for the Houston Buffaloes in the Texas League in 1930 and 1931 (Dizzy pitched 26–10 that second year and then moved up to his marvelous major-league career). Before going to the majors Mort Cooper pitched for Houston in 1938; his catcher was his brother Walker. Hall of Famer Rogers Hornsby and his older brother, Pep, played together in the Texas League. In 1934 twin brothers Clarence and Claude Jonnard were a battery for Fort Worth. Brothers Oyster Joe and Sam Martina played together at Beaumont, Texas, in 1912. All three Cruz brothers, Hector, Cirilo, and José, played for the Arkansas Travelers.

Minor-league players who became managers sometimes urged their parent clubs to sign their sons, who then played for them. In many cases, player-managers in their forties, particularly in the 1920s and 1930s, played alongside their sons, hitting behind them in the lineup. It was a

family tie that fans loved, a novelty hardly ever seen in the big leagues.

In smaller minor-league towns, the players, never paid much, usually lived in hotels or boarding houses or rented rooms in private residences. Unlike major leaguers in big cities, they became part of the community. They'd walk to the ballpark or take the streetcar like everyone else. Some hitched rides with fans who owned cars. Knowing they'd be with a

THESE THREE SHOWGIRLS FROM A BROADWAY REVUE CALLED *RAIN OR SHINE* SPENT THEIR VACATION IN FLORIDA, DATING MINOR-LEAGUE BALLPLAYERS THERE FOR SPRING TRAINING.

ALL KIDS HAD TO DO TO GET INTO THE BALTIMORE ORIOLES GAMES IN THE 1920S WAS STAND OUTSIDE THE PARK BEHIND THE MAIN TICKET GATE AT HOME PLATE. IT WAS A SINGLE-TIER PARK WITH A VERY LOW ROOF OVER THE HOME PLATE GRANDSTAND. THERE WERE NO CAGES THEN, AND DURING BATTING PRACTICE GUYS WOULD HIT LOTS OF FOULS BACK OVER THE HOME PLATE ROOF. ANY KID WHO CAUGHT A FOUL BALL AND TURNED IT IN AT THE TICKET WINDOW GOT A FREE TICKET FOR THE GAME. SOME OF MY FRIENDS USED TO HAWK FOUR OR FIVE BALLS BEFORE THE GAME AND GET THE WHOLE NEIGHBORHOOD IN FREE.

—MICHAEL KAWECKI,
OF BALTIMORE

team for several years, they'd sometimes take jobs in local stores to make ends meet in the off season. Many married local women, and some, having enjoyed seven or eight years of baseball in a town, later returned to make a home there.

In larger cities the success of teams on the field and at the box office meant the players were paid a little more and traveled better. They went by train, not bus, stayed at the best hotels on the road (a favorite was a posh hotel in Columbia, South Carolina, with a gorgeous indoor swimming pool), wore the finest suits, and dined at top restaurants. Some even went to spring training on cruise ships, with a bevy of showgirls from different New York revues and plays accompanying them. And everyone, but everyone, killed time by playing cards.

Owners not only wanted to keep players in those days, but could. The National Agreement inked back in 1901 called for payment of only $7,500 for any player the majors wanted to grab. Furious that top players were being taken away for that little money, the minors pulled out of the agreement in 1919. They re-signed it, but with a clause permitting them to get whatever they could negotiate in the sale of a player. That meant that in the 1920s a minor-league owner could keep stars for several years to build up their sale value. This enabled owners like Jack Dunn in Baltimore to put together a dynasty. It also enabled owners to earn substantial extra income, enough to save a franchise or make one prosperous, by selling stars.

The first big sales were of Willie Kamm and Jimmie O'Connell from the San Francisco Seals. O'Connell went to the New York Giants for $75,000 and Kamm to the Chicago White Sox for $100,000. The majors suddenly found they had to pay at least $50,000 to land a star minor leaguer. They also found owners holding on to players as the prices escalated. The practice made major-league owners fume and often enraged the players. Lefty Grove, for example, was by 1923 the best pitcher in the minors. The Philadelphia A's tried to buy him, but Baltimore's Jack Dunn held out for more money. He held out again in 1924 and again in 1925, rejecting pleas from a desperate Grove, who saw his chances at a shot in the majors slipping away. Finally, in 1926, Dunn drove the price on Grove up to $100,000 and sold him. (Grove went on to win three hundred games in the majors and always felt that if Dunn had not held him back for those few years he could have won close to five hundred.) Dunn also sold Jack Bentley, Max Bishop, and several others for another $200,000.

Ballparks, many of them built of wood at the turn of the century, had begun to dry and rot by the 1920s, becoming tinderboxes. Many burned down. Some teams played a

PLAYERS USUALLY STUCK TOGETHER ON THE ROAD. THIS GROUP IS
ON ITS WAY TO DINNER IN CHARLESTON, SOUTH CAROLINA.

summer in another town while the old park was rebuilt, but some left and never came back. Others, in smaller markets, were never well financed and after a few years, despite decent crowds, simply went out of business. Others, having lost the best players to major-league raids earlier, or to major-league money later, had enough bad seasons in a row to kill attendance for good and folded. Other teams would do so well that an entrepreneur in another city would purchase them and move them to his own backyard.

From about 1908 to 1930, despite general success, the minors saw many leagues start up and fail. The Dakota League started in 1921 and stumbled through just two seasons before folding. The Eastern Canada League started in 1922 and died in 1923. Indiana teams had a run of bad luck: The Indiana-Ohio League, started in 1907, died in a season; and the Indiana-Michigan League, started in 1910, lasted only one year. The Anthracite League, a Pennsylvania coal-country league, folded after one season in 1928, taking baseball away from little hamlets like Mount Carmel and Hazelton. The Arkansas League and Atlantic Association both started in the spring of 1908 and folded in the fall of 1908. Ohio's Buckeye League, bringing small-town baseball

NEWARK BEARS MANAGER WALTER JOHNSON (LEFT) GREETS NEW YORK GIANTS SKIPPER JOHN MEBRAM BEFORE A SPRING-TRAINING GAME IN 1926.

to Findlay (where Zane Grey played earlier), Lima, and Marion in 1915, collapsed after one season. The Iowa State League, started in 1911, lasted just six weeks. The Ontario League, in Canada, lasted just four, until 1930. Some teams folded in bad times, revived themselves in good times, then went under again. Duluth, Minnesota, in the Northern League, played from 1902 to 1905 and went out of business. It returned in 1908 for one year and folded again. The team came back in 1913 and played through 1916, then dropped out again. A generation later, in 1934, another entrepreneur brought a team back to Duluth and kept it going until 1942. The war ended that effort. A team came back to Duluth again in 1946 and played through 1955.

The 1920s would not end on a high note. As the decade roared to a close all of America was jolted by the stock-market crash. People with no jobs had no money and people with no money did not buy tickets to baseball games. The minors tumbled. There were twenty-five prosperous minor leagues in the United States, with nearly two

THESE PLAYERS FROM THE FINANCIALLY STRAPPED SPRINGFIELD (MASSACHUSETTS) PONIES, OF THE NEW ENGLAND LEAGUE, 1932, WENT BACK AND FORTH TO THE BALLPARK IN THE CAR BEHIND THEM.

WHEN I WAS A KID IN NASHVILLE IN THE MID-1920S, I USED TO SEE THE GAMES AT THE SULPHUR DELL PARK. WE DIDN'T HAVE ANY MONEY, BUT MY COUSIN, WHO WAS 21, WORKED AS A LINEMAN FOR THE PHONE COMPANY. THERE WAS A BIG TELEPHONE POLE RIGHT BEHIND THE LEFT-FIELD FOUL POLE. HE'D HELP ME GET UP IT WITH HIS LINEMAN'S STRAP AND WE'D SIT ON THE CROSSBAR ALL AFTERNOON AND WATCH THE GAME. BEST SEAT I EVER HAD.

—JOHN SADLER,
OF NASHVILLE, TENNESSEE

hundred teams, in 1929. By 1931, as unemployment soared to 25 percent and bread lines got longer, the number of leagues dropped to just sixteen, and those sixteen struggled. Owners and players fretted. Little did they know that the same forces that plagued them in the 1920s, the major-league owners arguing over player costs, and the Great Depression itself, would save them and hurtle them into their glory years.

THE PACIFIC COAST LEAGUE:
THE THIRD MAJOR LEAGUE

The three-thousand-mile distance from the East Coast to California did not deter the grizzled miners in the gold rush of 1849, but it was too much for major-league baseball. The majors ignored the distant West Coast until 1958. It didn't matter much to West Coast baseball fans, though. They didn't need a major league: They had the Pacific Coast League. With teams owned by movie stars, franchises near casinos, earthquakes knocking over stadiums, the longest seasons in sports, higher salaries than the majors, and opening day parades led by boxing champions, West Coasters were hardly deprived the excitement of big-league ball.

Good baseball was being played throughout the Pacific coast area even before the Civil War. By the turn of the century, three strong West Coast

OAKLAND STADIUM IS FILLED TO
CAPACITY FOR THE
1948 CHAMPIONSHIP SERIES.

BALL TEAM
-1890-

leagues were attracting thousands of fans as well as the support of local businessmen. Fan loyalties were strong. When the Oakland G & M's would play the Sacramento Solons, players and fans would pile onto sturdy riverboats to make the trip. The PCL debuted in 1903 with franchises in Los Angeles, Sacramento, San Francisco, and Oakland, California; Portland, Oregon; and Seattle, Washington. The PCL expanded continually over the years. The

THIS 1890S OAKLAND TEAM, WHICH PLAYED IN THE CALIFORNIA LEAGUE, WAS RATHER STYLISH. ITS PLAYERS WERE PAID ABOUT EIGHT DOLLARS PER GAME.

league went international with a Vancouver franchise in 1956; Hawaii joined in time for the 1961 season; and in the 1960s and 1970s the league added teams from Arizona, Colorado, and Indiana, and two more teams in Canada. The PCL has had franchises in thirty-three different cities in thirteen states and Canada, making it geographically the largest minor league and earning it the moniker the "Third Major League."

The Pacific Coast League has been hit with many storms over the years but with dedicated owners and supportive fans has managed to survive all of them. After a successful organization in 1903, the league was nearly devastated when the great San Francisco earthquake of 1906 destroyed both its ballparks in that city. In World War I the whole league shut down, and a decade later the Depression hurt everybody. In 1958 the PCL shuddered when the major-league Dodgers and Giants moved to California, kicking the Seals and Angels right out of town and knocking other PCL teams off their perches for several years. When Anaheim, San Diego, and Seattle landed major-league franchises in the 1960s and 1970s, the PCL suffered even more. Still, fine players, good business people, and loyal fans continued to support the PCL, and in the 1970s and 1980s it grew to be strong once again. Today the league has prosperous franchises in Albuquerque, New Mexico; Colorado Springs, Colorado; Las Vegas, Nevada; Phoenix and Tucson, Arizona; Portland, Oregon; Tacoma, Washington; Vancouver, British Columbia; and Calgary and Edmonton, Alberta.

The Pacific Coast League has always been different from other leagues. For one thing, it has had glitz and glamour like no other league has ever enjoyed. After all, with a team called the Hollywood Stars, owned by real Hollywood stars, how could it not be bathed in glamour? Right from the start, movie stars

A 1941 PACIFIC COAST LEAGUE RECORD BOOK SHOWS TONY LAZZERI'S 60 HOME RUNS AND 222 RBIS FOR THE 1925 SEASON.

THE STARS WERE EAGER TO GET THEIR GAMES ON THE AIR WHEN TELEVISION BEGAN BROADCASTING BASEBALL IN THE EARLY 1950S.

MANY FILM CELEBRITIES HELD STOCK IN THE HOLLYWOOD STARS, AND PROGRAMS OFTEN RAN PHOTOS OF MOVIE STARS. EDDIE CANTOR APPEARS INSIDE THIS 1948 PROGRAM.

fell in love with baseball. Fatty Arbuckle, the silent-screen comedian, was president of the Vernon Tigers, one of the two Los Angeles teams, in 1919 when they won the pennant. Later, in the 1930s, celebrities Barbara Stanwyck, Gary Cooper, Gene Autry, Bing Crosby, William Powell, George Burns, and Gracie Allen were stockholders of the Hollywood Stars, owned by Bob Cobb. (Cobb also owned the illustrious Brown Derby restaurant; board meetings were held there or on some star's yacht.) Liz Taylor was once a team cheerleader. Movies funny man Joe E. Brown pitched in the final game of the 1935 season. Stars were always seen at games at Gilmore Field. Ballplayers were "discovered," just like starlets, in Hollywood. Chuck Connors, who spent a year with the Dodgers and Cubs, then played in the PCL for Los Angeles, was at bat in the 1952 season when a television producer, looking for a new face to star in Westerns, spotted him. Convinced Connors's tough, chiseled face was what he needed, he coaxed him away from the backstop and on to the back lot. Connors, a decent hitter, became a television star with his own long-running hit Western, "The Rifleman."

The PCL has also boasted some of the finest and most interesting stadiums

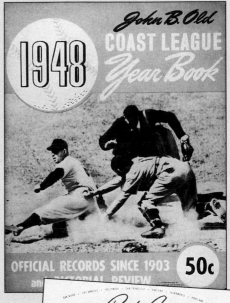

The Pacific Coast league issued colorful and comprehensive yearbooks.

The Pacific Coast league even had its own newsletter for fans.

Padres pitcher Al Benton and Rainiers outfielder Clarence Maddern grace cards issued by Mother's Cookies in the late 1940s and early 1950s.

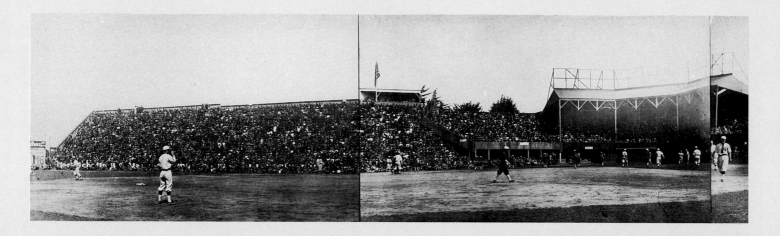

THIS PHOTO IS A COMBINATION OF THREE PICTURES TAKEN BY A NEWSPAPER PHOTOGRAPHER AT FREEMAN'S PARK, OAKLAND, IN 1911. THE STANDS ARE JAMMED TO CAPACITY, AND YOU CAN SEE, ON THE FAR LEFT, THAT HUNDREDS OF FANS SAT ALONGSIDE THE FOUL LINES AND IN THE OUTFIELD. IN THE MIDDLE, STUCK ON TOP OF THE GRANDSTAND LIKE A CORK, IS THE PRESS BOX.

in the country. The 18,600-seat Seals Stadium was built in San Francisco in 1931 at the then-astronomical cost of $600,000. It had three clubhouses—one for the Seals, one for the visiting team, and one for the Missions, another PCL team that used the ballpark. In 1945 shipping magnate Paul Fagan bought the Seals and was determined to get them into the National or American League with a fancy ballpark. He installed baseball's first glass backstop so fans could see perfectly, built the first deluxe press box, spent thousands to create gorgeous women's rest rooms to build up female attendance, hired baseball's first nattily attired female ushers, hired golf groundskeepers to improve the grass turf, and made the clubhouses the poshest in the country. In 1926 William Wrigley, the owner of the Chicago Cubs, decided to invest in the minors and bought the Los Angeles Angels (he owned an estate on Santa Catalina Island, twenty-six miles out from Los Angeles). He promptly built spectacular Wrigley Field (it didn't seem to bother him that his Chicago ballpark carried the same name), with its lovely high clock tower (which housed Pacific Coast League offices) and Spanish architecture, at the unheard of cost of one million dollars. Sportswriters of all leagues immediately dubbed it the prettiest park in America.

Distance has also set the PCL apart from other leagues. Until the late 1950s, most PCL franchises were more than 1,500 miles from the nearest major-league city, Saint Louis. The PCL played its games in splendid isolation, a very big fish in its own very big pond. The league had West Coast psychology on its side. Separated by days of travel until the advent of the jet airplane in the

1960s, the West Coast developed its own culture and its own lifestyle, and the PCL was its own, very precious, league.

With good year-round weather, PCL teams used to play a long, 200- to 225-game season (144 these days). They heavily promoted their series and games, bringing in such figures as boxing champ Jim Jeffries, race-car whiz Barney Old-field, and amphibious movie star Esther Williams to throw out the opening-day ball or serve as grand marshals of opening-day parades. Team owners, many of them involved in various local civic organizations, still make certain there are reduced rate tickets for kids, hospital patients, and the underprivileged.

The real key to the longtime success of the Pacific Coast League, though, has been the policy of keeping popular teams together for years to build fan support. The dynasties of the league, like the San Francisco Seals of the 1920s and Los Angeles Angels of the 1930s, showed fans the same familiar faces year in and year out.

In keeping the same teams, and putting them on the field more than two hundred times a year, owners have made the ballplayers a part of community life (and thus helped build attendance). In the glory years, the 1930s and 1940s, the teams generally paid hefty salaries to attract and keep players. They used money to lure major leaguers just finishing careers to play several more seasons in the PCL, promoting them as gate attractions. The league paid players a minimum of $5,000 a year—the same as the major-league minimum—and in many cases more. Today, as a Triple "A" League, the PCL gets many talented players who soon move up to the majors.

In the early years, the league was filled with top former major leaguers who enjoyed the climate, the lifestyle,

ONE OF THE FINEST BALLPARKS ON THE WEST COAST AT THE TURN OF THE CENTURY WAS RECREATION PARK, IN SAN FRANCISCO. IT WAS DESTROYED IN THE 1906 EARTHQUAKE, ALONG WITH ANOTHER PACIFIC COAST LEAGUE PARK, AND THE TEAMS HAD TO PLAY OUT THE SEASON ELSEWHERE.

VIEW FROM CITY HALL LOOKING SOUTH DOWN 8TH ST — 1896 —

the nice working conditions, and the money. Lefty O'Doul, a San Francisco native, is a good example. A superb pitcher and hitter, he played for San Francisco in 1918 (with a 12–8 pitching record), then jumped to the New York Yankees, where he saw little action in two seasons. He came back to the Seals in 1921 and had a 25–9 record and hit .338. He went back to the Yankees, then Red Sox, but played little. Frustrated, he went back to the PCL, playing for Salt Lake City, where he hit .392 in 1924, .375 in 1925, and .338 in 1926, when the club moved to Hollywood. In 1927 he went home, to San Francisco and the Seals, hit .378, stole forty bases, and was the PCL's Most Valuable Player. The majors realized their mistake and lured him back. He spent the next seven years with the Giants, Phillies, and Dodgers. He was sensational, winning the National League batting title in 1929 with a sizzling .398 average; hitting .383 in 1930; and winning another batting crown in 1932 with a .368 mark. His batting average for those seven years in the majors was .349.

THIS TACOMA LEOPARDS BALLPLAYER TAKES TIME OUT FROM BATTING PRACTICE TO POSE. THIS PHOTO, TAKEN AROUND 1928, SHOWS THE FLIMSY ONE-TIER GRANDSTAND COMMON AT MANY BALLPARKS.

But O'Doul missed the PCL and when he had an offer to return in 1935 as player-manager of the Seals he jumped at it. The Seals had a lot to offer: more money than he could ever make in the majors ($50,000 a year), a chance to live in his hometown, and such benefits as good weather and better traveling conditions.

The Pacific Coast League also nurtured players who hadn't excelled in their flings with the majors for various reasons but performed well in the West. Jigger Statz, who played more minor-league games than any other player in minors history and became a PCL legend, played two seasons with the New York Giants and Boston Red Sox, seeing just spot action. In 1920 he played part of the winter with Los Angeles in the PCL to stay in shape. A wiry, five-foot-seven-inch, 150-pound hitter, he fell in love with the climate, the people, and the players in Los Angeles. He also learned quickly that he could make

THE 1938 TACOMA TIGERS TOOK A TRAIN TO MOST GAMES, BUT USED THIS CUSTOMIZED DOUBLE-DECKER BUS FOR SOME. THE WELL-FINANCED TIGERS ARE WEARING THEIR OWN SPECIALLY DESIGNED JACKETS. THEIR MANAGER, SECOND FROM RIGHT IN THE BACK ROW, IS FORMER MAJOR-LEAGUE HOME-RUN SLUGGER AND HALL OF FAMER HACK WILSON.

CHARLES DRESSEN
Oaks Team Manager

REMAR BREAD, A LARGE WEST COAST
COMPANY, ISSUED THESE PLAYER
CARDS OF THE OAKLAND OAKS IN
THE 1940S. THIS ONE IS OF CHARLIE
DRESSEN, OAKS MANAGER. LIKE
MANY PCL MANAGERS, HE HAD BEEN
A SKIPPER IN THE MAJORS, THOUGH A
DISASTROUS ONE (FINISHING EIGHTH
TWICE, SIXTH, AND FIFTH, WITH THE
CINCINNATI REDS FROM 1934 TO
1937). IN THE PACIFIC COAST
LEAGUE HE REFINED HIS SKILLS AND
DID SO WELL WITH OAKLAND THAT HE
WAS BROUGHT BACK TO THE MAJORS
BY THE DODGERS IN 1951. HE WENT
ON TO WIN TWO PENNANTS WITH THEM.

more money in the PCL than he could in the National League. He stayed for the next season, hitting .310, and went up to the majors again. He bounced around for a few seasons, hitting .319 for the Cubs one year, before returning to the PCL, where he became a Los Angeles fixture. Like so many other popular players in the league, he played into his forties.

The PCL also attracted major-league stars slightly past their primes, who traveled west to extend their careers at the good salaries offered there. In 1948 Oakland Oaks manager Casey Stengel convinced several former major leaguers, among them Eric Lombardi and Cookie Lavagetto, to play for him in the PCL. The recruits, dubbed "the nine old men" by the press, won the pennant for Casey.

Like all the minor leagues the PCL offered fans a chance to see young stars who would move on to true greatness in the majors. These included players like Paul Waner, Billy Martin, Tony Lazzeri (the first man to hit sixty home runs in professional baseball), Lefty Gomez, Gus Zernial, and Gene Woodling. The league's true superstars, both hometown boys, were Joe DiMaggio and Ted Williams. DiMaggio, who didn't play organized ball until he was seventeen, broke in with the San Francisco Seals in 1932 and played through 1935, when he moved up to the Yankees and history. Even buried in far-off California in the middle of the Depression, DiMaggio and his graceful fielding and fluid swing drew national attention. He had hits in each of sixty-one consecutive games in 1933, his first full year, and batted .398 in 1935. Farther down the coast, in San Diego, high-school superstar Ted Williams joined the San Diego Padres in 1936. He hit .271 that year, .291 with twenty-three homers the next, then moved up to the Boston Red Sox, where he became an immediate sensation.

Along with—or in spite of—its glitz and glamour, its seasoned major-league stars, and its young sensations, the PCL has always shown its fans good ball. The San Francisco Seals won five pennants in ten years from 1922 to 1931 and from 1922 to 1925 averaged 122 wins a year. The Los Angeles Angels, playing in magnificent Wrigley, posted an almost unbelievable record of 137 wins and 50 losses in 1934, making it one of the most powerful minor-league teams in history. Fans flocked to see the great teams play. Interest grew and by the 1940s, attendance was soaring; more than four million people saw PCL games in 1947. With the league's incredible success, some PCL leaders, led by the Seals' owner

Paul Fagan, tried to get baseball commissioner Hap Chandler to make the PCL a third major league.

Due to several factors, that never happened. Television hurt all minor leagues badly in the early 1950s, when major-league games suddenly became accessible to all. In 1958 the Dodgers and Giants moved from New York to California, smashing any hope of the PCL becoming a major league. Even so, through the years the PCL has proved over and over again that minor-league baseball can be as exciting and as glamorous as major-league ball. Attendance at PCL games jumped to 1.6 million in 1979 and to 2.3 million in 1989. Attendance climbed to more than 2.7 million in 1992, when many PCL teams pulled 300,000 fans or more for the season. The players who went from game to game on riverboats back in the 1890s would be proud.

THE ZEE NUT CANDY COMPANY PRODUCED A LINE OF BASEBALL CARDS JUST FOR THE PACIFIC COAST LEAGUE. THESE 1913 CARDS FEATURED SAN FRANCISCO SEALS PLAYERS HOGAN AND GADREAU.

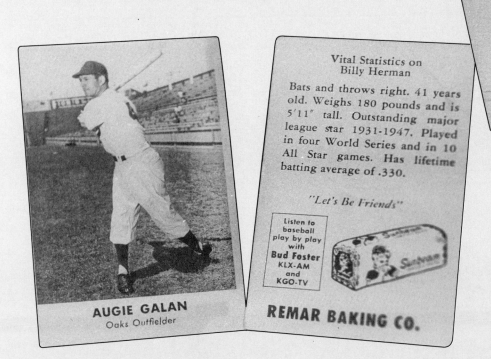

AUGIE GALAN
Oaks Outfielder

Vital Statistics on
Billy Herman

Bats and throws right. 41 years old. Weighs 180 pounds and is 5'11" tall. Outstanding major league star 1931-1947. Played in four World Series and in 10 All Star games. Has lifetime batting average of .330.

"Let's Be Friends"

Listen to
baseball
play by play
with
Bud Foster
KLX-AM
and
KGO-TV

REMAR BAKING CO.

AUGIE GALAN WAS A TYPICAL OLDER PLAYER IN THE PCL. HE PLAYED IN THE MAJORS FOR FIFTEEN YEARS AND HIT A RESPECTABLE .287. HE THEN MOVED TO CALIFORNIA AND PLAYED ON INTO HIS FORTIES IN THE PCL.

DAVENPORT BLUE SOX, 1933

COMPLIMENTS of IOWANA FARMS MILK CO.

THE THINGS A BALLPLAYER HAD TO DO: THE DAVENPORT BLUE SOX PLAYERS,
SEEN HERE IN A 1933 PHOTO, HAD TO HAWK IOWANA FARMS MILK.

CHAPTER FOUR

DOWN ON THE FARM

Branch Rickey looked like anything but a baseball man. He was nattily and fastidiously dressed, always in a suit, and players joked that he slept in one. He wore thin-rimmed glasses that accentuated his bushy eyebrows. He was not only a college graduate, but a college professor, and if all that didn't prove he was smart, he had a law degree and was a lawyer. He didn't want to practice law, though. He preferred his other job as the general manager of the greatest baseball team in the world—the Saint Louis Cardinals, who won the world championship in 1926, placed second in 1927, and took the National League pennant again in 1928. They were on top of the world. Everybody thought the Cards would dominate the National League forever. Rickey was the only skeptic. He had a world championship and two pennants when the 1930s opened, but he had a problem.

Rickey knew that the wholesale selling of stars by the minor leagues had hurt the Cardinals. The Cardinals were a cash-poor team and could not pay $100,000 to get three players, much less one Lefty Grove. The current system, which the minors thrived on, helped only rich teams like the Yankees and the Giants and the Athletics. Poor teams, like the Cards, would soon be unable to compete. Rickey took the saying "If you can't beat them,

join them," one step further: "If you can't beat them, control them."

With the blessing of club owner Harry Breadon, Rickey secretly began buying up interest in minor-league teams. His plan was to find good, young ballplayers and put them on minor-league teams the Cardinals owned, then move them up when they were trained and ready for major-league ball. Whatever money the Cards would spend buying minor-league teams would be money well spent: The team would save $100,000 each time they wanted to bring up the best players. "The Mahatma," as he was called for his law degrees and wisdom, started buying teams in 1921, quietly—no sense letting everybody else in on a good idea. He bought several more in 1926. By 1931 the Cardinals owned sixteen teams outright. But that was not enough for Rickey—he just kept going. He would buy 100 percent of a club one month, then 51 percent and controlling interest of another the following month. He collected minor-league teams like other people collect coins. Ten, fifteen, twenty, and on up. By 1940 the Cardinals owned the controlling interest in thirty-three minor-league teams, or a tenth of all the teams in the country. The Cards owned 51 percent of most, but a full 100 percent of fifteen teams. Rickey soon owned half the Nebraska State League and half the Arkansas-Missouri

League. Then he bought up the rest of the teams in each league. All told, the Cardinals had a farm system of some five hundred players from which to choose new talent each year. And not one of them, when moved to the majors, would cost the front office a nickel. (Baseball commissioner Kenesaw Mountain Landis later ruled the ownership of entire leagues a monopoly and broke them up.)

The scheme worked well. The Cards' first big-city team, the Rochester (New York) Red Wings, won International League pennants every year from 1928 to 1931. Rickey plucked his next Card's manager, Billy Southworth, from the Red Wings. Rickey's first acquisition in the Pacific Coast League was an interest in the Sacramento Solons. From that club the Cards acquired Pepper Martin, a key cog in their championship teams in the 1930s. Dizzy Dean was spotted toiling on one of the Cards' farm teams and —not quite ready for the big time—was sent down to another of their teams, in the Texas League, where he was

BRANCH RICKEY, GENERAL MANAGER OF THE ST. LOUIS CARDINALS, BEGAN THE MAJOR LEAGUES' FIRST "FARM SYSTEM" OF MINOR-LEAGUE TEAMS.

A QUICK GLANCE AT THIS 1928 INTERNATIONAL LEAGUE SCHEDULE SHOWS WHAT A LONG SEASON THE TEAMS PLAYED—168 GAMES THAT YEAR, 14 MORE THAN THE MAJOR LEAGUES. THEY OFTEN PLAYED FIVE OR SIX GAMES A WEEK.

OFFICIAL 1928 SCHEDULE INTERNATIONAL LEAGUE CHAMPIONSHIP

	AT TORONTO	AT BUFFALO	AT ROCHESTER	AT MONTREAL	AT READING	AT BALTIMORE	AT JERSEY CITY	AT NEWARK
TORONTO	**The Star-Eagle**	May 29, 30† A. M. and P. M. July 3, 4‡ A. M. and P. M. 29† Aug. 5†, Sept. 16†, 21, 22*, 23†	May 18, 19*, 20†, 21 June 3†, 25, 26, July 1†	May 25, 26*, 27†, 28 July 22†, 23, 24, 25 Sept. 2†, 10, 11, 12	April 26, 27, 28* June 9*, 10†, 11, 12 July 15†, Aug. 19, 14, 15, 16	April 29-25†, 30, May 6-8† June 18, 14, 15, 16* Aug. 18*, 19-19†	April 22†, 23, 24, 25 May 13-13†, June 17† 18, 19, 20 22*, 24† Aug. 10, 11*, 12-12†	April 18, 19, 20, 21* June 17† 18, 19, 20 22*, 24† 26†
BUFFALO	May 22, 23, 24† A. M. and P. M. July 26, 27, 28* and P. M. Sept. 14, 15*	**Presents**	June 5, 6, 7, 8 July 22†, 23, 24, 25 Sept. 2†, 10, 11, 12	June 2*, 3†, 4‡ A. M. and P. M. June 29, 30*, July 1‡ July 22 A. M. and P. M. Sept. 17, 18, 19	April 22†, 23, 24, 25 June 13, 14, 15, 16* Aug. 17, 18-18*, 19†	April 18, 19, 20, 21* June 9*, 20†, 11, 12 Aug. 13, 14, 15, 16	April 26, 27, 28* June 17-17†, 18, 19 20 Aug. 7, 8-8, 9	April† 29†, 30, May 1 24† Aug. 10, 11*, 12-12†
ROCHESTER	June 1, 2-2* July 22 A. M. and P. M. Sept. 6, 7, 8-8*	May 25, 26*, 27†, 28 Sept. 31 A. M. and P. M., 4-6	**Complete**	May 22, 23, 24† June 19, 20* July 26, 27, 28*, 29† Sept.†20, 21, 22*, 23†	April 29, 10-30 June 17†, 18, 19 20- 30 Aug. 7, 1-8, 9	April 26, 27, 28* June 31, 33, 22*, 24† 24† Aug. 10, 11*, 12-12†	April 18, 19, 20, 21* June 13, 14, 15, 16* Aug. 17, 18†, 19-19†	April 22†, 23, 24, 25 June 9*, 10†, 11, 12 Aug. 13, 14, 15, 16
MONTREAL	June 5, 6, 7, 8 July 22†, Aug. 1, 2 Sept. 31 A. M. and P. M., 4, 6	May 18, 19*, 20†, 21 June 25, 26, 27, 28 Sept. 6, 7, 8*, 9†	May 20, 30† A. M. and P. M. July 3, 4‡ A. M. and P. M., 6 Aug. 4*, 6†, Sept. 16*, 16†	**Baseball**	April 18, 19, 20, 21* June 11, 12, 22*, 24† July 10, 11-11*, 12†	April 22†, 22, 24, 25 May 22, 23, 24, 25 P. M. Sept. 2-3†, 24-25*	April 28-25†, 30 June 9*, 10-10†, 11 12† Aug. 13, 14, 15, 16	April 26, 27, 28-28* June 13, 14, 15, 16* Aug. 17, 18*, 19-19†
READING	May 14, 15, 16, 17 July 14-14*, 16, 17 Aug. 27, 28, 29-29	May 10, 11, 12*, 13† July 10, 11, 12, 13 Aug. 30, 31, Sept. 1-1	May 4†, 5, 6, 7 July 18, 19, 20, 21* Aug. 20, 21, 22, 23	May 2, 3, 4, 5† July 18, 19, 20, 21* Aug. 24, 25*, 26-26†	**Information**	May 22, 23, 24, 25 July 4‡ A. M. and P. M. Sept. 2-3†, 24-25*	May 18, 19*, 20-20† July 22†, 23, 24, 25 Sept. 14, 15*, 16-16†	June 5, 6, 7, 8 June 29-30*, July 1†, 2† Sept. 10, 11, 12, 13
BALTIMORE	May 7, 8, 9-9 July 18, 19, 20, 21 -21 Aug. 30, 31, Sept. 1*	May 3, 4, 5-5 July 6, 7*, 8†, 9 Aug. 26, 27, 28, 29-29	May 14, 15, 16, 17 July 10, 11, 12, 13 Aug. 24, 25†, 26-26†	May 15, 16, 17†, 18 July 14*, 15†, 16, 17 Aug. 27, 28, 29-29	May 30† A. M. and P. M., 31, June 1 July 30, 31, Aug. 1, 2 Sept. 3‡ A. M. and P. M., 4, 5	**for the Fans**	May 26*, 27-27†, 28 July 26, 27, 28*, 29† Sept. 14, 15, 16	May 10, 11, 12*, 13† June 25, 26*, 27, 28 Sept. 6, 7, 8, 9†
JERSEY CITY	May 10, 11, 12-12* July 10, 11, 12, 13 Aug. 20, 21, 22, 23	May 14, 15, 16, 17 July 15, 16, 20, 21 Aug. 24*, 25, 26-26†	May 3, 4, 5, 6 July 14*, 15†, 16, 17 Aug. 30, *31, Sept. 1-1	May 4†, 7, 8, 9 July 6†, 7*, 8†, 9 Aug. 27, 28, 29-29	June 2*, 3†, 4‡ Aug. 4*, 6†, 9† Sept. 7, 8*, 9†	June 5, 6, 7, 8 1-1† Sept. 10, 11, 12-13	**Every Day on**	May 24, 25, 30† D. M. P. M., 31 Sept. 3‡ A. M. and P. M., 22*, 22-23†
NEWARK	May 2, 3, 1, 5* July 8, 6, 7-8 Aug. 14-24, 25-25*	May 6†, 7, 8, 9 July 14*, 15†, 16, 17 Aug. 20, 21, 22, 23	May 14, 15, 16, 17 July 18, 19, 20-21 Aug. 27, 28, 29-29	May 10, 11, 12*, 13† July 10, 11, 12, 13 Aug. 30, 31, Sept. 1-1	May 15*, 17†, 18, 29 June 25, 26*, 27, 28† Sept. 27, 28, 19, 29	June 2*, 3-3†,4 Aug. 4†, 5-5†, Sept. 16*, 16†	May 22, 23, 24 A. M. June 1 July 3, 4‡ A. M., 6 Aug. 1, 2 Sept. 3-3‡, 4, 11	**Sport Pages**

* Denotes Saturdays   † Denotes Sundays   ‡ Denotes holidays

ALLENTOWN, PENNSYLVANIA, CENTER FIELDER GEORGE HESSE WENT TWO FOR FOUR AGAINST ALBANY, NEW YORK, IN THE EASTERN LEAGUE ON MAY 9, 1929, BUT HIS TEAM LOST ANYWAY, 14–9.

BUDDY HASSETT CAME INTO THE MINORS IN 1933 AS A FIRST BASEMAN IN THE YANKEE CHAIN. HE SOON BECAME THE STARTING FIRST BASEMAN FOR THE BROOKLYN DODGERS, HITTING .303 OVER HIS FIRST THREE YEARS.

groomed to become a legend. The list of talent pulled from the Cards' pool went on and on.

Jacob Ruppert, the millionaire owner of the Yankees, admired Rickey for his genius. If the cash-poor Cardinals could develop a farm system that stretched from coast to coast, why not the Yankees, who had lots of money? In 1931 Ruppert crossed the Hudson River and bought the Newark Bears, plus their stadium, which he promptly renamed Ruppert Stadium. Then he bought teams in Kansas City, Kan-

sas; Binghamton, New York; Norfolk, Virginia; and Akron, Ohio, and had working agreements or part ownership of ten other teams, including Joplin, Missouri; Basset, Virginia; Rogers, Arkansas; and Butler, Pennsylvania. The Yankees also owned part of the San Francisco Seals. By 1939 the Yanks controlled two hundred minor-league players. Within a decade, the Newark Bears alone had sent over a dozen starters to the Yankees, including Charlie "King Kong" Keller, Joe Gordon, Red Rolfe, and George Selkirk.

IN 1933, MY FIRST YEAR, IN WHEELING, WEST VIRGINIA, MY MEAL ALLOWANCE PER DAY WAS SEVENTY-FIVE CENTS. WE MANAGED TO FIND A LUNCHEONETTE IN TOWN WHERE YOU GOT A WHOLE MEAL, ENTREE, COFFEE, AND DESSERT—THE WORKS—FOR A QUARTER. WHENEVER I HEARD OF PEOPLE SPENDING A DOLLAR FOR DINNER I THOUGHT THEY WERE RICH.

—BUDDY HASSETT, WHO PLAYED IN THE MINORS BEFORE JOINING THE BROOKLYN DODGERS

Ruppert and Rickey had opened the floodgates. Seeing the benefits of outright ownership of "farm" clubs, just about every other big-league team started buying up minor-league teams. The Brooklyn Dodgers, one of the most woeful teams in the majors in the 1920s and 1930s, embarked on a buying spree that would bring them total or partial ownership of twenty minor-league teams by 1947, including the Montreal club in which Jackie Robinson broke the color line. The Dodgers had so many minor leaguers that at spring-training tryouts in the late 1940s, where players were assigned numbers, many had three digits on their backs.

THE COLUMBUS, OHIO, REDBIRDS OF 1935.

HARTFORD, CONNECTICUT, FIELDED TEAMS IN THE CONNECTICUT STATE LEAGUE, EASTERN
ASSOCIATION, AND EASTERN LEAGUE FROM 1902 TO 1932. THESE PLAYERS WERE ON THE
1930 HARTFORD TEAM, A VICTIM OF THE DEPRESSION TWO YEARS LATER.

Fortunately, the majors' ownership and investment in teams (which would grow in later years) had a stabilizing effect on the minor leagues, and by the mid-1930s the leagues were healthier than ever. When the buying of teams began, the minors themselves, stunned by the Great Depression, were starting to climb back. They had a long way to go. In the summer of 1931, for example, Bob Irelan, owner of the Quincy, Illinois, team in the Three I League, reported average ticket sales of just seven hundred per game. Weekend games in the Eastern League were pulling just five hundred fans. Many club budgets were so tight that fans were asked to return home-run or foul balls they caught (in exchange for a ticket for the next game). Judge William Bramham, head of the Piedmont League and president of the national minor-league association, lead the resurgence of the minors. He was convinced that if the

AS IN MOST CITIES, ONE OF THE STREETCAR TERMINALS IN
LOUISVILLE WAS AT THE BALLPARK. BASEBALL GAMES
WERE SO LUCRATIVE FOR STREETCARS THAT THE RAILWAY
COMPANIES WERE ABLE TO DEMAND CONSTRUCTION OF
STADIUMS AT SITES ON THE LINE.

> IN THE 1930S THE STREETCAR LINE IN
> LOUISVILLE ENDED RIGHT AT PARKWAY
> FIELD. EVERYBODY RODE THE STREETCAR TO
> THE GAME—TEN CENTS A RIDE, THREE FOR
> A QUARTER. DURING THE GREAT DEPRESSION,
> MY DAD WOULD TREAT US BY TAKING US TO THE
> BALL GAMES ON THE STREETCAR. THOSE RIDES
> TO PARKWAY FIELD, AND THE TIME WE HAD, ARE
> SOME OF MY BEST MEMORIES.
> —ROSEMARY TEXAS, OF LOUISVILLE, KENTUCKY

good relations with the press and promoting all of minor-league ball.

Promotions started to appear. During the Depression, fans could get dishes at the ballpark, just as they could at the movies. Ladies' Days were marketed heavily. For one highly hyped Ladies' Day in Rochester, New York, the Red Wings took on Toronto in the first game and played their major-league parent club, the Saint Louis Cardinals, in the second. The Red Wings sold fifteen thousand tickets that day, more than twelve thousand of them to women. More teams started knothole gangs, providing kids with free season tickets (attendance was so bad for struggling teams that the kids made up half the crowd on some afternoons). The Springfield, Massachusetts, *Daily News* began its own "Sandlot League," in which kids whose parents bought the paper got discounted tickets. Some team owners started handing out free blocks of season tickets to local schools, which then distributed them to students with good report cards. Many small-town teams, financially marginal as the Depression spread across the land, began to hold "Old Timers'"games, inviting former stars back for a game against the current team. To keep player morale up, owners sometimes split the proceeds from a single game (often an exhibition against a major-league team) with the squad as a "bonus."

Aware that the touring Kansas City Monarchs were carrying around a portable lighting system to play night baseball, Bramham urged minor-league owners to install permanent lights on the roofs of their stadiums, so workers who could not get to day games could still see their teams play. The first game with permanent lights was played on May 2, 1930, in Des Moines, Iowa. Within weeks, dozens of minor-league ballparks had permanent lights, and by the end of the summer more than a hundred did. The

minors kept ticket prices low, turned their ballparks into entertainment centers, and marketed themselves through innovative promotions, they could survive the Depression. He got most clubs to hire public-relations directors to lead their campaigns. His own office did the same, establishing

Hampdens Move Fast To Rout Bulldogs, 12-1

Springfield Gets 13 Hits For 22 Bases and Makes Four Double Plays as Schulster Scores First Win

BY J. EARL CHEVALIER

The New Haven Bulldogs didn't have a single snarl left at League park yesterday afternoon, when the Springfield Hampdens got through with them. Hitting sharply in spots and fielding expertly enough to add four double plays to an already large quantity, the Home city collection scored a convincing 12 to 1 triumph and pushed the Bulldogs further into the cellar. At the same time young Billy Schulster, Hampden right-hander, accounted for his first mound victory of the season.

Dreesen Comes Through

Fittingly enough, the white-haired boy who batted in the first of Springfield's dozen runs yesterday was Billy Dreesen. The applause of the spectators had barely floated away in the breeze at the time Dreesen, reappearing on the diamond where he built a reputation good enough to send him to the majors, drilled a single in the opening inning to register Joe McGuire, on third base by virtue of his own and Luke Urban's scientific hit to right. Moreover, Dreesen served as middle man in three twin-killings and set a fourth in motion.

"Buzz" Phillips started for the Bulldogs only to be smitten so smartly in the first inning that Manager Gene Martin didn't dare send him back to the peak. The Hampdens collected three runs in the initial frame. At the expense of Al Mahon and "Coke" Woodman they fashioned a cluster of six in the third stanza, when Nolan, Smith and Schulster authored genuine bingles to mix with bases on balls and a lone error. Woodman yielded three more runs in the seventh as Urban, Dreesen and Stapleton hit for extra bases.

The three New Haven mound ca[...]

dates granted 13 hits for a total of 22 bases and gave 11 passes in all. On the other hand Schulster allowed only seven safeties and passed two. Lehman's triple, which carried beyond the head of McGuire when Joe raced in and Bill Barrett's swift single scored New Haven's run. The score:—

SPRINGFIELD (EL)

	ab	r	h	po	a
Helgeth, 3b	4	1	0	2	7
McGuire, cf	5	2	2	1	0
Urban, rf	4	3	3	0	0
Dreesen, 2b	4	1	2	9	4
Hohman, lf	4	1	1	6	0
Stapleton, 1b	1	1	1	11	0
Nolan, ss	5	1	1	0	7
Smith, c	4	1	2	3	0
Schulster, p	5	1	2	0	0
	37	12	13	27	18

NEW HAVEN (EL)

	ab	r	h	po	a
Parenti, 2b	4	0	1	2	4
Lehman, 3b	4	1	1	2	0
Barrett, ss, 1b	4	0	2	7	1
Caldwell, 1b	2	0	0	3	0
Curry, ss	2	0	0	2	0
Walsh, c	4	0	1	3	0
Nason, rf	4	0	2	0	0
Scholz, cf	3	0	0	2	0
Straub, lf	3	0	0	2	0
Phillips, p	0	0	0	0	1
Mahon, p	1	0	0	1	1
Woodman, p	2	0	0	0	0
	31	1	7	23	9

Springfield ... 3 0 6 0 0 0 3 0 — 1[...]
New Haven .. 0 0 0 0 0 1 0 0 0 —

Runs batted in, Dreesen 3, Stapleton 2[...] [Ur]ban, Hohman, Schulster, Bar[...] [...]han, Dreesen, Staple[...] [...] hits, Ur[...]

Aug 30 1934 OFFICIAL BASEBALL

SCORE CARD 5c

BELMAR BRAVES
BASE BALL CLUB
MEMORIAL FIELD, F Street at 12th Avenue, BELMAR, N.J.

This 1930 newspaper clip from Springfield, Massachusetts, is a good example of the snappy writing by sportswriters for small-town papers, which devoted a huge amount of space to the town's minor-league team.

The Belmar Braves were a lower-level minor-league team that played a long schedule for the entertainment of summer vacationers at Belmar, a small resort town on the New Jersey shore.

Waldo Shank, a Toledo car dealer, owned the Toledo Mud Hens and talked his players into sitting in cars in his showroom to draw customers.

THE SECOND PLAYER FROM THE LEFT IN THE FIRST ROW OF THIS TEAM FROM
SING SING PRISON IS THE FABLED ALABAMA PITTS, THE HARD-HITTING OUTFIELDER
WHO CAUSED A NATIONAL UPROAR WHEN HE WAS SIGNED BY THE ALBANY SENATORS
UPON HIS RELEASE.

lights boosted attendance considerably. (Even so, the major leagues did not install lights until 1935.)

The coming of night baseball pumped new life into teams throughout the Southwest, Texas, and the plains states of Kansas, Oklahoma, and Nebraska, where insufferable temperatures, often topping one hundred degrees Fahrenheit in the afternoon, kept attendance down at day games. By the mid-1930s most Texas League teams used lights for night baseball, and attendance soared. At a time when the only buildings with air-conditioning in most towns were movie theaters or fancy hotels, people went to ballparks, now lighted, to beat the heat at night. Cool breezes blowing through open-air grandstands (few parks were completely enclosed) gave fans relief from the oppressive heat.

In another tact, the minor leagues began to make playoffs lengthy affairs to build interest and increase revenue. Bramham approved the so-called Shaughnessy playoff system, invented by Montreal Royals general manager Frank Shaughnessy in 1932, which pitted the top four, not two, teams in leagues against each other in playoffs. Teams also divided their seasons into two eight-week parts, with the winner of each part playing the other at the end of the year. This created interest in the playoffs and prohibited any team from running away from the rest. Gradually, business got better and then, slowly, great.

By the early 1940s there were forty-three minor leagues and more than 350 teams. New leagues included the Evangeline League, Penn State Association, Alabama-Florida League, Coastal Plains League, North Carolina State League, West Texas-New Mexico League, Mountain State League, Pioneer League, Pony League, and Tar Heel League.

Ironically, the Depression contributed to the success of the minor leagues in the 1930s, when more than 25 percent of Americans were unemployed. Every small town and city had bread lines and shelters. People sold apples and pencils in Amarillo just as they did in New York. As the gloom of the Depression spread, people looked for ways to escape the blues. Many found refuge in movies and baseball. Movie moguls produced so many films to satisfy a people looking for escapism that small-town theaters from coast to coast could show a new film—sometimes two—every week. Knowing that money was tight, theaters kept ticket prices low and counted on volume—nightly they were packed.

I WAS A TYPICAL YOUNG BALLPLAYER IN 1938. SEVENTEEN YEARS OLD, HIGH SCHOOL SENIOR, DRAFTED BY THE DETROIT TIGERS AND SENT TO PLAY FOR ALEXANDRIA, LOUISIANA, IN THE EVANGELINE LEAGUE. A GUY FROM THE TEAM PICKED ME UP AT THE BUS STATION AT 4 A.M. AND DROVE ME TO AN OLD BOARDING HOUSE THE TEAM USED. MY ROOM WAS A SMALL CELL WITH A TINY BUREAU, A SMALL LIGHT BULB DANGLING FROM THE CEILING, AN ARMY COT, AND NO DOOR. I COULD HEAR TEN MEN SNORING AND WAS DETERMINED NOT TO STAY THERE. I LEFT AND FOUND THE BALLPARK, GOT INTO THE CLUBHOUSE THROUGH A SMALL WINDOW, PUT TWO LONG WOOD BENCHES TOGETHER, AND MADE A PILLOW OUT OF MY CLOTHES. NO MATTER WHAT HAPPENED NOW, I KNEW I WAS SAFE FROM EVERYTHING AT THE BALLPARK.

—HAL NEWHOUSER,
LATER A HALL OF FAME PITCHER

Minor-league baseball used the same tactics. Trying to win back crowds, owners wisely kept ticket prices low, usually a quarter or thirty-five cents. Most teams hired a public-relations director to get more coverage in newspapers. The pregame and game stories that got into the local press helped stress the role of teams as members of their communities. This made it easier for a team to work out promotional deals with local businesses, solicit advertising for their outfield fences and programs, and get help

FLOYD "LEFTY" ISEKITE PLAYED BALL FOR THE TACOMA TIGERS, THEN IN THE WESTERN INTERNATIONAL LEAGUE, WHERE HE THREW A NO-HITTER IN 1937. HE MOVED ON TO THE PACIFIC COAST LEAGUE IN 1940.

PETE GRAY ONLY HAD ONE ARM, BUT HIS HITTING PROWESS, AND THE ABILITY TO FIELD ADROITLY BY ROLLING THE BALL ACROSS HIS CHEST, WON HIM A SHOT IN THE BIG LEAGUES WITH THE SAINT LOUIS BROWNS IN 1945. HE WAS SENT DOWN TO THE MINORS IN 1946, WHERE HE PLAYED FOR ANOTHER SIX YEARS.

from local government. (City and town maintenance crews often included groundskeeping around ballparks as part of their work day. City councils eased zoning restrictions to permit minor-league stadiums to build parking lots. Community groups helped find low-rent rooms or apartments for players.) By 1933, as Franklin D. Roosevelt took office, minor-league baseball began to be seen as the same kind of escape valve as the movies.

Team owners could not afford to be generous, and life for their players could be hard. The money was pathetic. Salaries were as low as $175 a month, and meal money was tight. Players would often study the local newspapers to find community picnics or fairs where food was inexpensive. Many ballplayers could only afford to rent rooms in rooming houses or in private homes. Widows, eager to have a young man around the house to make them feel safe and help with chores, often took in ballplayers as boarders.

Teams often got around in school buses that were too old to safely transport students. Many low-level minor-league teams couldn't even afford those. They went from town to town in leased cars. The entire team—players, equipment, and administrative office—would often squeeze into two cars, luggage strapped to the top, duffel bags stuffed with bats tied to the running boards. Alta Cohen, who

THE BALLPARKS WERE PUT WHERE THEY FIT, SOMETIMES AWKWARDLY. THIS PARK WAS SUPPOSED TO FIT SNUGLY ON A CITY BLOCK, BUT WHEN IT WAS BUILT A TELEPHONE POLE WAS IN THE WAY. THE PHONE COMPANY DIDN'T WANT IT REMOVED, SO IT REMAINED.

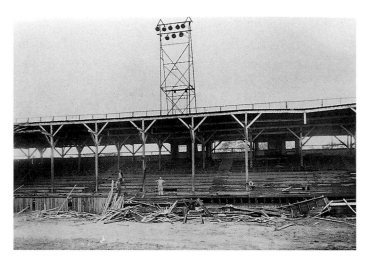

BY THE 1940S MANY BALLPARKS BUILT AT THE TURN OF
CENTURY HAD BURNED TO THE GROUND. LAUER PARK, IN
READING, PENNSYLVANIA, REMAINED STANDING BUT IN
1944 WAS IN SUCH BAD SHAPE THAT THE CITY TORE IT
DOWN. ANOTHER PARK OPENED IN 1951.

played with the minors through the late 1920s and early 1930s before moving up to the Dodgers, remembers that sometimes only half the team would make it to the game. "Your infield would be in the dugout and your outfield would still be out on the highway," he recalls.

Everybody played baseball in the 1930s. Schools, factories, and railroads all fielded teams—and there were even teams behind bars. Prisons all over the United States entered a new era in the 1930s. Direct punishment was being downplayed and rehabilitation stressed. Classes were offered, convicts were given productive jobs (including that old reliable—making license plates), and athletics were considered to be a useful part of rehabilitation. A main prison yard was the size of a baseball field, and it was easy for prisons to erect temporary backstops and bleachers from which convicts could watch prison teams play one

another. To spice it up, wardens at many prisons invited semipro, minor-league, and even major-league teams into the prison to play the convicts. San Quentin's warden would make a whole day of it, with a game followed by an elaborate dinner for visiting teams, with printed programs. Several wardens allowed the players out of jail to travel, with a bevy of guards, to a nearby town for a game.

Most of the prisoners on these teams were decent ballplayers who had played in high school or on sandlots, but in the 1930s word began to leak out of Sing Sing, in Ossining, New York, that there was a player so good he could play in the major leagues. His name was Edwin "Alabama" Pitts, and he was serving five years for armed robbery. With Pitts in the lineup and the outfield the Sing Sing team consistently beat visiting teams. No records were

THE MEMPHIS STEAM LAUNDRY COMPANY WAS LOCATED RIGHT BEHIND THE LEFT AND CENTERFIELD WALLS AT RUSSWOOD PARK IN MEMPHIS. THERE WERE FOUR SMALL SMOKE-STACKS OVER THE LEFT-FIELD WALL, ABOUT 350 FEET FROM HOME PLATE, AND ONE TALL ONE IN DEAD CENTER, ABOUT 450 FEET OUT. BIG COLUMNS OF STEAM WOULD POUR OUT OF THEM. IF A BATTER HIT THE ONE IN CENTER THE STEAM LAUNDRY WOULD PAY HIM $1,000. IF HE HIT THE ONES IN LEFT, HE'D GET $200. THE STACKS WERE NARROW, SO THE LAUNDRY PEO-PLE FELT PRETTY SAFE ABOUT THEIR OFFER. WELL, ONE SUMMER IN THE LATE 1940S, A SLUGGER NAME BILL WILSON HIT THEM ALL SO MANY TIMES HE EARNED HIMSELF $4,200—AS MUCH AS HE MADE PLAYING BASEBALL.
—JOHN HUDSON, OLIVE BRANCH, MISSISSIPPI

kept of the prison ball games, and prisoners' names were never used in the stories that appeared in local papers, but teams who played inside Sing Sing's walls said the mercurial slugger hit close to .400 every year.

Pitts was released in 1935. He was immediately signed by the Albany team of the International League. Bramham, of the minor-leagues' national association refused to okay the deal, feeling Pitts' presence would create a bad image for the minors. He was also fearful that Albany would use him as a gimmick to build up the gate. In fact, there were rumors that Albany was a straw man for a major-league team that wanted Pitts to boost its sagging attendance. Pitts argued that the prison system existed to rehabilitate people, and a convict who became a good ballplayer in prison and could earn a living at it when he got out was a success story. Bramhan refused, and Pitts, no fool, had friends take his case to the newspapers, which howled that he was a victim

BABY-FACED PEE WEE REESE IN HIS LOUISVILLE UNIFORM. REESE WENT ON TO A HALL OF FAME CAREER IN THE MAJORS.

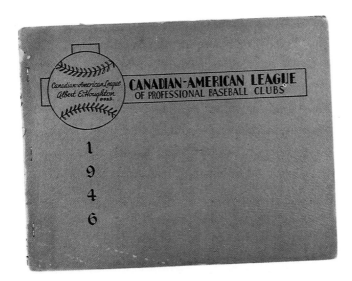

WORLD WAR II SHUT DOWN THE CANADIAN-AMERICAN LEAGUE FROM 1942 TO 1946; THIS IS THE LEAGUE'S FIRST POSTWAR RECORD BOOK.

of the prison system. If Pitts could play baseball, editorials trumpeted, he would be an inspiration to every other inmate. The uproar became so great that Bramham, shrewd politician that he was, dumped the controversy in the lap of Judge Landis, the baseball commissioner. Under a barrage of public opinion and hounded by reporters, Landis ducked the issue for weeks. He conducted an investigation that showed, he said, that Pitts had been in numerous scrapes with the law over the years and was a temperamental man with a short fuse (at the time, though, the Associated Press reported, his armed robbery conviction—he stole seventy-two dollars from a department store—was his only run-in

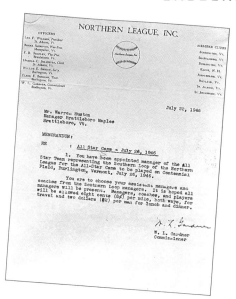

One of the most remote minors circuits was the Northern League in New England. This letter from league commissioner Bill Gardner reminded managers to keep expenses down for the annual all-star game.

Players before the 1946 Northern League all-star game.

with the police). Landis, and others, worried that on the road he might wind up killing somebody in a bar fight or be killed himself. The press attention would not subside. Thousands of VIPs across the country wrote letters in support of Pitts; among his supporters was the manager of the department store he had held up in 1930. Eventually, Commissioner Landis carefully explained that Bramham and his minor-league colleagues were, of course, right, but the fact remained that a contract was a contract, and if Albany wanted to sign anybody, well, who was he to stop them.

Pitts was signed and started the year hitting at a solid .280 clip, bringing out large crowds wherever Albany played. Ticket sales grew at town after town as Alabama Pitts and his Albany team blew into the area. The hard-working Pitts, who had played so well against everybody in prison, even hitting consistently off the Yankees when they visited, could not sustain a long season of minor-league ball and constant travel. His average fell slowly as the season progressed. The phantom major-league club so intent on signing him lost interest. The ex-con played for Albany for forty-three games, hitting just .233, before he was demoted to a lower-level league, where his batting average fell even more. He played on in the lower minors for five seasons. He died on June 7, 1941, in Valdese, North Carolina, in a bar fight.

For minor-league teams fan loyalty remained a constant. Fans would follow their team everywhere. If baseball was outlawed in one town because of Sunday blue laws (many cities—even whole states—had them to stop the sale of liquor or prevent athletic events from being held), teams simply played in another town. Fans didn't care. They just wanted to see their team play ball.

Leo Murphy, now eighty, who saw many games as a kid growing up in Scranton, Pennsylvania, remembers:

HOME OF LOUISVILLE COLONELS

THE MAJORS HAD THE WORLD SERIES AND THE MINORS HAD THE JUNIOR
WORLD SERIES, WHICH PITTED THE CHAMPS OF THE A LEAGUES AGAINST
EACH OTHER. THESE FANS ARE STREAMING INTO PARKWAY FIELD,
LOUISVILLE, TO CATCH THE 1945 JUNIOR WORLD SERIES.

Because of blue laws, which forbade baseball in Scranton on Sundays, the team traveled to Artillery Park, a two-thousand-seat wood ballpark next to the U.S. Army's artillery depot in Old Forge, maybe five miles outside town, where there were no blue laws. It was such a ragtag park that the outfield fences were the removed sides of railroad boxcars. Every summer the Pittsburgh Pirates would play an exhibition game against Scranton at Artillery on Sunday so the players, who couldn't play in Pittsburgh on Sunday, could make some extra money. There must have been ten thousand people jammed into and around that little ballpark every Sunday they came out to get around the blue laws.

Tiny ballparks began to dot the country as more and more leagues sprang up and survived into the late 1930s and early 1940s. Ballparks were built wherever owners could fit them. One entrepreneur realized when he laid out his park on paper that a telephone pole would be right next to first base, but he built it anyway. In a park in the Midwest, a railroad track ran behind the left-field wall. When a train started to pull in or out during a game, fans would start to yell, and the batter would turn to aim at left field. When

> WHEN I WAS A KID THE LOCAL MINOR-LEAGUE TEAM USED TO HAVE HUNDREDS OF TICKET CONTESTS. YOU KNOW, NAME THE FIRST PRESIDENT AND WIN A PAIR OF TICKETS TO THURSDAY'S BALL GAME. IT WAS RIDICULOUS, BUT THERE WAS SORT OF A CHARM TO IT AND EVERYBODY WOULD ENTER THESE TICKET CONTESTS. YOU NEVER SAW SO MANY PEOPLE PROUD OF WINNING TWO BUCKS WORTH OF TICKETS.
> —JOE DEFAZIO, 63, OF WAPPINGERS FALLS, NEW YORK

one hit a passing train the stands broke out in unrestrained jubilation. The ballpark in Louisville, Kentucky, was constructed at the same time as Eastern Parkway, which ran right past it. It was named Parkway Field, and over the years sluggers hit dozens of cars zipping past the left-field wall. Beach Park, home to a Houston, Texas, minor-league team, was built along the Gulf of Mexico, and the right-field fence was on the edge of the beach. One day a player hit a home run over the fence, but a high tide, surging in as the player trotted slowly around the bases, swept the ball back under the fence and into right field. The right fielder picked it up, and his throw beat the runner to the plate (he was ruled safe after a long argument). Fort Worth's Panther Park was constantly being flooded by the Trinity River. The park burned down on May 15, 1949, and the next day, you guessed it, what remained was under four feet of water when the Trinity overflowed. A ballpark on an island in the Connecticut River near Brattleboro, Vermont, was swept away in a 1940 flood.

The owners of the team in Beckley, West Virginia, had a real dilemma—the only place they could build their stadium was on top of a cliff. A high wooden wall guarded left field—just beyond it was a straight drop of four hundred feet ("It was one place you didn't try to catch home-run balls," said a left fielder who played there). The International League ballpark in Baltimore actually had a maintenance shed in deep left field. One day a bouncing line drive headed for the shed and the worker leaning against it, watching the game. The ball bounced inside the shed's open door, and the worker, seeing a chance for some runs to score, slammed the door shut and would not let the outfielder retrieve it. Perhaps one of the strangest minor-league parks was in Austin, Texas. Before 1896, when the local team, the Senators, leased it, the ballpark had been home to a circus. The circus tent came down but, to save money, the two circus bleachers under the tent were left intact; home plate was simply placed between them. Then the field was built, giving Austin America's only three-ring ballpark. Another park in Austin had its name, Disch Field, carved into the outfield grass so everybody knew the name of the man who owned it. Redbird Stadium in Columbus, Ohio, had the largest scoreboard in the minors, running almost fifty feet high and two hundred feet wide. The owners of the ballpark at Johnstown, Pennsylvania, could not afford standard kleig lights, so they illuminated their field by stringing sets of automobile headlights from telephone poles. Dudley Field, in El Paso, Texas, set up a mammoth venetian blind at the rear of the stands to protect fans from the hot sun. Dudley's center field rose ten feet, and the canal running behind it would flood the outfield when it overflowed its banks.

Interest in the minors grew until the start of World War II, when the departure of several million men for the war, gas rationing, restrictions on train travel, and a general gloom in the country once again slammed shut minor-league coffers, just as World War I had done. But in the postwar years the minors picked up just where they left off. The players were back from the war and eager to make up for lost time. Recently discharged servicemen jammed as much entertainment into their lives as they could to make up for lost time, and that included minor-league baseball. Major-league teams, anticipating a surge in postwar attendance, poured more money into the development of their minor-league partners.

The charm remained. The intimate relationship fans had always had with minor leaguers—the intimate rela-

MINOR LEAGUERS ALWAYS WENT OUT OF THEIR WAY TO POSE FOR PICTURES WITH FANS, ESPECIALLY KIDS. HERE "BOO" FERRIS, WHO WOULD GO ON TO A SIX-YEAR CAREER WITH THE BOSTON RED SOX FROM 1945 TO 1950, POSES WITH A BRATTLEBORO, VERMONT, BOY IN 1941.

tionship that they could never have to the same degree with major leaguers—grew stronger. Barry Halper, a part owner of the Yankees who was a Newark Bears fan in the late 1940s, remembers, "It was like going down to the store to see people you knew. You could call anybody over to the rail and talk to them. You got millions of autographs. I would trade things I had for their shirts, pants, cleats, and started to build a collection. Other kids would find out what buses or trains they took home, get on and sit with them—every day. They were your heroes, but they were your friends, too."

The minors continued to grow. The Newark Bears thrived and so did the nearby Jersey City Giants, packing the crowds into cavernous Roosevelt Stadium, where Jackie Robinson made his debut in 1946 with Montreal (he broke the color line in style, with four hits in four at bats). From 1946 to 1949 the Pacific Coast League set new attendance records each year. By the late 1940s more than forty million Americans were watching minor-league games a year, and baseball became bigger than ever in Canada.

For years, the minors played the so-called Junior World Series between different A-level league winners. Perhaps the 1944 Junior World Series, between the Orioles and Louisville, was the best barometer of how big minor-league ball was. Game four, at Baltimore, drew 52,833 fans, more than the major-league World Series in Saint Louis drew that same week. Orioles manager Tommy Thomas told an interviewer years later:."The police chief told me they were afraid of a riot when so many people jammed the gates, so they just let another 8,000 or so in, unpaid, so you really had some 60,000. It was amazing."

Operating a lower-level minor-league team in the 1940s was not limited to the rich, as most think, and teams thrived because ownership was easy. Letters recently uncovered by New Hampshire historian Bob Lowell show that the operation of a team was no more expensive than running a local hardware store. In a prospectus for the revival of the New England League, mailed in 1940, orga-

nizer Claude Davidson, who finally got the league going six years later, listed every imaginable cost for an owner.

Players' salaries (entire team)	$ 8,500
Manager's salary	2,000
Park rental (10% of expected 40,000 person gate at 50 cents a ticket)	2,000
League dues (for costs and umpires)	2,000
Transportation	500
Hotel ($3 per day per player)	1,350
Meals (60 cents per day per player)	324
Uniforms ($20 per, home and away, 17 men)	680
Baseballs (600)	500
Training expenses	600
National Association fee	75
Total	$18,529

Revenue, Davidson promised prospective owners, would come from crowds, expected to average 750 per game (more on weekends, less on weeknights), at 50 cents per ticket, for $22,000. That gave each owner a profit of $3,471 —plus, Davidson emphasized, profits from concession stands, exhibition games, radio, and the lucrative outfield fence billboards. Revenue would come in weekly and be used to pay bills. The only up-front money an owner would have to put up was the franchise fee, which was just $250.

A year after Davidson's first efforts, while the league was still in the planning stages, one of its other organizers, Thomas Fleming, wrote a prospective owner and told him he could secure lights for his ballpark, cheap, find him top players, and get some financial help. Later, in 1945, the winter the league started, Fleming was guaranteeing prospective owners that he could land former major-league stars like Wally Schang of the Yankees and Smoky Joe Wood of the Red Sox as managers. Fleming again promised to get top players, and reminded owners of an added source of revenue.

"1 know that Mr. [Connie] Mack will send us good players. With Class A, then if you have a player good enough to be drafted, then the majors must pay [at least] $6,000 for each player," wrote Fleming, dangling the carrot all owners coveted. After all, the sale of one player to the bigs for $6,000 would double an average operating profit.

Governor Francis Murphy of New Hampshire, a lover of baseball who thought it would be fun to own a team, tried to buy into the Boston Braves in 1940. Failing that, he began targeting minor-league teams, and that year bought

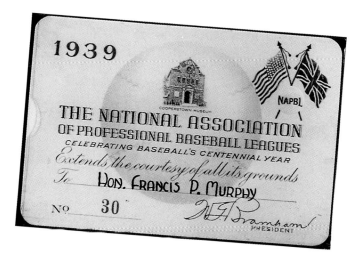

THE NATIONAL ASSOCIATION ISSUED LIFETIME PASSES TO MANY PROMINENT POLITICIANS. GOVERNOR FRANCIS MURPHY OF NEW HAMPSHIRE BOUGHT A BASEBALL TEAM OF HIS OWN.

MY FATHER WAS KILLED IN A MINE COLLAPSE AND I HAD TO GET A JOB TO HELP THE FAMILY, SO I GOT ONE IN A REFRESHMENT STAND AT THE SCRANTON RED SOX BALLPARK IN 1938. WE GOT COMMISSION. SODA WAS A DIME AND SO WAS A HOT DOG. OUR CUT WAS A PENNY FOR EACH. WHEN SCRANTON TOOK ON WILKES BARRE, THE BIG LOCAL RIVALRY, THE PLACE WAS PACKED. I'D MAKE TEN DOLLARS A DAY! THE REAL MONEY WASN'T IN THE SODA, THOUGH, IT WAS IN THE EMPTY WOOD CARTONS THE SODA CAME IN. THE SCRANTON WILKES-BARRE GAMES ALWAYS PULLED A SELLOUT CROWD AND THE OWNERS WOULD LET ANOTHER TWO-THOUSAND OR SO PEOPLE SIT ON THE OUT-FIELD GRASS. MY BUDDIES AND I WOULD TAKE ALL THE EMPTY SODA CAN CARTONS AND RENT THEM TO PEOPLE AS OUTFIELD SEATS FOR FIFTY CENTS EACH. WE MADE A FORTUNE!

—BILL TROTZ,
OF WILKES BARRE, PENNSYLVANIA

interests in two New Hampshire ball clubs. The word was out that Murphy was a serious investor, and clubs came running. In the spring of 1945, when Davidson and others, including sportswriter Bob McGarigle of the *Boston Herald*, were in the final stages of putting their New England League together, Murphy was invited to their meeting and then heavily courted by them. They even went so far as to offer him the presidency of the league and a job for his son if he bought a franchise. Fleming waffled but did finally buy a team in the league.

In 1949 there were a record fifty-nine leagues, 464 teams, and ten thousand players in minor leagues in the United States Attendance was a record 41.8 million. The minors, in size, scope, and drawing power, had become major at last. Like the cocky warrior running across the beach without looking, the minors were headed for a series of land mines. The 1950s would bring minor-league baseball to the brink of ruin.

THE WONDER TEAM: THE NEWARK BEARS

CATCHER BILL SKIFF,
WHO WENT ON TO A FINE MAJOR-
LEAGUE CAREER, STANDS WITH TEAM
BUSINESS MANAGER WILBUR CRELIN
(CENTER), WHO RAN THE TEAM FROM
A NEWARK STOREFRONT.

T he Newark Bears were the wonder team of all baseball in 1937. They had loyal fans, a good stadium, and played outstanding baseball. They were the kings of the minors.

The Bears began as the Domestics in 1884, playing in the Eastern League. Hall of Famer Joe McGinnity, who had earned his fame with the New York Giants, arrived as owner, manager, and pitcher in 1909, and under him the Bears won twenty-nine games that year and thirty the next. The Bears won the International League pennant in 1913, playing in spacious Weidemeyer Park, an old wooden stadium that seated ten thousand. In 1915, though, the new Federal League put the major-league Peppers into the Bears hometown. The Peppers would probably have lost to the Bears in any game they played, but the Peppers were the major league. They drew crowds of fans away from the Bears.

The Bears were abandoned. Business was so bad they left town and played the 1914 season in Harrisburg, Pennsylvania. They came back when the Federal League, and with it the Peppers, folded a year later. Weidemeyer Park burned down in 1925, forcing the Bears into a nomadic existence again. They played their home season in Providence, Rhode Island. In 1926 they moved into a new stadium in Newark and in 1928 acquired a new owner, Paul Block, the social lion who published the *Newark Star Eagle* and several newspapers in New York.

Block spared no expense, sending his ballplayers to spring training in Florida on cruise ships, putting them up in the best hotels on the road, and buying the best equipment available. He promoted the team ceaselessly (he gave away thousands of tickets to school kids), headed up a drive to put finishing touches on the new stadium, and involved the whole community in the Bears' future.

The Depression crippled Block's business empire, as it did so many others. Desperate for money, in 1931 he sold the Bears to Yankees owner Jacob Ruppert. The new owner modestly named the ballpark Ruppert Stadium and

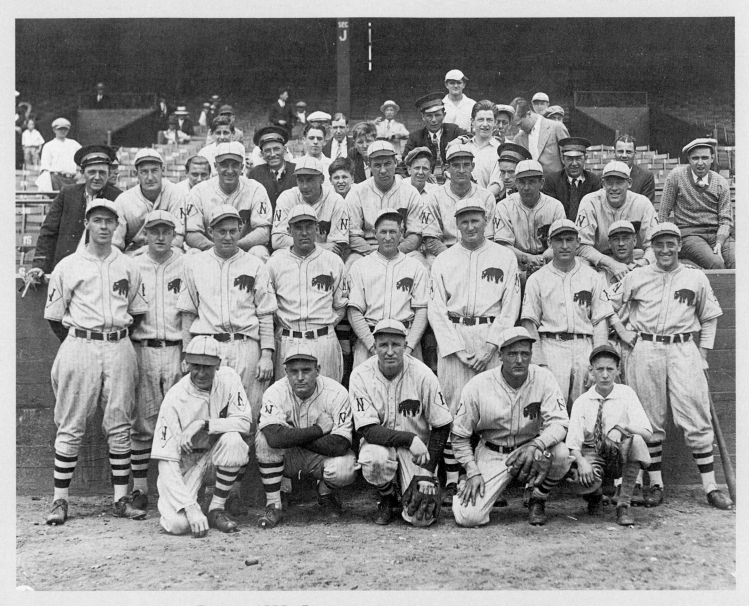

THE LATE-1920S BEARS HAD CUBS SEWN ON THEIR JERSEYS.
NOTE THE USHERS WHO SNEAKED INTO THIS TEAM PICTURE.

began stocking it with ballplayers he bought from other teams or signed to lucrative contracts right out of high school.

The 1930s were glory years for the Bears and for Newark baseball fans. The Newark Eagles, one of the best teams in the Negro Leagues, arrived in 1937 and leased Ruppert Stadium on days the Bears were not using it. Black superstars such as Roy Campanella, Satchel Paige, Cool Papa Bell, Josh Gibson, and Buck Leonard came to town regularly.

The Bears gained strength under Ruppert and drew sizable crowds to Newark, New Jersey's largest city and in that era one of America's most prosperous. Newark then had a thriving business district, with several legitimate theaters, an opera house, ballet companies, and a long string of movie houses. Newark was in the

ALL MINOR-LEAGUE CITY NEWSPAPERS RAN FULL-PAGE PHOTO SPREADS OF THE PLAYERS NEAR OPENING DAY. THE NEWARK STAR EAGLE PULLED OUT ALL THE STOPS AND DISTRIBUTED A THIRTY-SIX-PAGE SPECIAL SECTION ON THE BEARS (MAYBE THAT'S BECAUSE THE NEWSPAPER PUBLISHER OWNED THE TEAM).

THE BEARS WON THEIR OPENER, 6–0, IN 1928, BUT WENT DOWNHILL FROM THERE, FINISHING SIXTH.

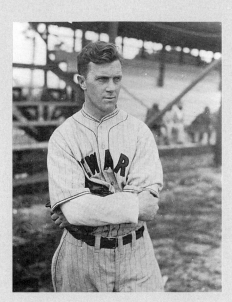

MIKE MARTINECK CAME TO THE
BEARS IN THE LATE 1920S FROM
HARRISBURG, PENNSYLVANIA, WHERE
HE LED THE NEW YORK–PENN LEAGUE
IN HITTING WITH A .366 AVERAGE.

CHICK DAVIES

MAJOR-LEAGUE STAR WALTER
JOHNSON, ONE OF THE GAME'S
MOST POPULAR PLAYERS, RETIRED TO
BECOME MANAGER OF THE BEARS
IN 1928. HE HOLDS A MINIATURE
BEAR HERE.

middle of the northern, most populous part of the state and easy to reach by rail lines.

"We'd jump on a train in Boonton and be in Newark in half an hour," says lifelong baseball fan Tony Marcello, who saw dozens of Bears games when he was a kid. "The ballpark was a ten-minute walk from the train station. You'd run for the train and be home forty minutes after the game ended. Going to see the Bears was the easiest thing in the world."

The Bears won pennants in 1932, 1933, and 1934, and then in 1937 fielded what was said to be the best minor-league team of all time. They had Charlie "King Kong" Keller, a devastating slugger ignored by other teams who thought he had no potential. Keller, nicknamed for his burly physique and thick eyebrows, hit .353 that season and in 1939 moved up to the Yankees, where he became a star. Another reliable player was Jimmy Gleeson, who went on to hit .333 with the Chicago Cubs in 1940. Joe Gordon, who went to play for the Yankees for seven years and won the 1942 Most Valuable Player award, anchored an infield that included George McQuinn, who played twelve years in the majors, Babe Dahlgren, and Buddy Rosar. The pitching staff included Atley Donald, Joe Beggs, Steve Sundra, and Vito Tamulis. Collectively they won seventy-three games and lost only sixteen. Donald's record was 19–2.

"None of the pitchers was overpowering, but they had a nice variety of pitches that were hard to hit," says Marius Russo, a rookie hurler for the Bears that year who also played for the Yankees. "They all had tremendous control." Asked at the time what made Charlie Keller such a great slugger, manager Ossie Vitt replied, "I don't know what he's got, but I wish I had it."

The Bears scored six runs in the first inning of the first game of the 1937 season, letting the International League know what was ahead. They went on to win 109, lose just 42, and win the league title by 25½ games. They won the Junior World Series and were welcomed home in Newark's biggest parade ever. Every single starter, the manager, and all but one of the backup players went on to the major leagues.

The modern world caught up with the Bears, though. The Lincoln and Holland tunnels and the George Washington Bridge, all connecting New Jersey to New York, were built in the 1930s, making it easy for fans to get into the Big Apple to see the New York Yankees, the New York Giants, and the Brooklyn Dodgers. After World War II, Newark residents began their exodus to the suburbs. Television, with many stations in the New York area, hurt, too. In 1949 the once-vaunted Bears were drawing fewer than seven hundred fans a game, and in 1950 they shut their gates forever.

"It was a sad day," says Buddy Hassett, their last manager. "The Bears were part of life in Newark for seven decades."

They'll live in memory, forever, though, as they were in the splendid summer of 1937—as the greatest team minor-league baseball ever saw.

PITCHER BILL SEHULSTER

WALTER JOHNSON AND ROOKIE PITCHER
BILL SEHULSTER IN 1928.

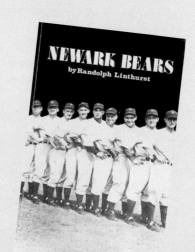

THE NEWARK BEARS WERE SO POPULAR THAT
FIVE DIFFERENT BOOKS WERE WRITTEN ABOUT
THEM. THIS IS ONE OF THREE WRITTEN BY
RANDOLPH LINTHURST. THE POWERHOUSE
1937 TEAM GRACES THE COVER.

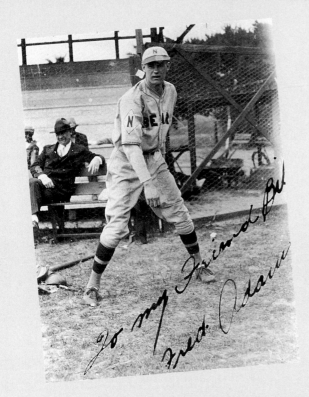

Fred Adams

Bill Skiff

Pitcher Al Mamaux
works out.

Pitcher Marty Phelin

HUNDREDS OF FANS WELCOMED THE DALLAS EAGLES HOME AT UNION STATION, DALLAS, AFTER A 12-7 ROAD TRIP THAT MOVED THEM TO WITHIN A GAME OF FIRST PLACE IN JUNE 1951.

CHAPTER FIVE

THE FALL

Bob Murphy, the radio broadcaster for the New York Mets, leaned back against the wall of his tiny, two-tier broadcast booth at Shea Stadium recently and looked at the television camera in the next booth. "On radio," he explained, "the listener can't see anything, so I use words to paint a picture of what the stadium, the people, the game looks like. On television, there's little to be said. The camera shows you absolutely everything. On radio, everything is left to the imagination. On television, nothing is."

Radio broadcasts of major-league games became popular in 1937, when the Cincinnati Reds' broadcasting network began to operate in several states, bringing Cincinnati baseball to millions. The radio games whetted people's appetites for the real thing. People heard the games and began going to the ballparks, major and minor, to see the real thing. By 1949 more than four hundred local radio stations were carrying minor-league games, helping boost attendance at ballparks across the country. Minor-league owners assumed television, which started broadcasting baseball in the late 1940s, would help them even more. They were fatally wrong. TV did just the opposite. Why trudge on down to the stadium, or in some areas drive an hour or take a train, to see a game you could watch in your own home? Why go watch

your local minor-league team when you could see major leaguers play from the comfort of your living room? Television not only penetrated the baseball market; it saturated it. By the summer of 1950 there were 225 television stations coast to coast carrying the "major league game of the day." Some carried other major-league games, too, and fans in some areas could see five different major-league games in a single day—and this was in television's primitive days, before cable and satellite dishes.

Television's impact was devastating. With so much baseball on television, attendance at minor-league parks dropped from a high of 41.8 million in 1949 to 34.5 million in the 1950 season, then to 27.5 million in 1951, and continued to plunge. The major-league teams, of course, greedy for the television dollar, did little to restrict the impact of the new media on their minor-league affiliates. This error would haunt them in years to come.

Television wasn't the only villain chipping away at the strength of the minors. Manufacturers of air-conditioning units were able to refine their technology and increase mass production to sell relatively cheap window units that the average family could afford. People no longer had to seek out air-conditioned theaters or the breeze-swept stands of baseball stadiums to stay cool on hot summer days.

A SMALL GRANDSTAND, TYPICAL OF A SMALL-TOWN BALLPARK OF THE 1950S, SITS BEHIND THE MANAGER OF THE GENERALS TEAM IN THE NORTHERN LEAGUE.

Little League, designed to get everybody interested in baseball and create an audience of kids who would later flock to the ballpark, helped put the minors in a coma. Little League became enormously popular in the 1950s, especially in rural towns where the minors once thrived. Parents started going to their children's Little League games two or three times a week, leaving little time to go to a local minor-league game.

The late 1950s and early 1960s saw the beginning of large seashore and lake developments, also luring away baseball fans. "The summer they opened Old Hickory Lake, a huge manmade lake, we lost everybody," says John Sadler, a former owner of the Nashville Volunteers, which shut down in 1961 after sixty years. "We went down to maybe a hundred people a game. Everybody in town was out at Old Hickory swimming or on water skis. We had to go out of business."

By the middle of the 1950s Americans were watching three or four hours of television a day. With free entertainment of all kinds on television, from baseball to Milton Berle, who needed to pay the price of admission to a minor-league ballpark? The mid-1950s also saw the success of rock-and-roll music, pulling a large segment of the teenage audience away from the minors. The evolution of technicolor movies, three-D, and Cinerama lured more and more families to movie theaters.

Baseball, which had a virtual monopoly on spectator sports for a century, now had to fight off competing sports, too. College football, always popular, now became even more so, and television brought many Saturday afternoon games into the living room. Professional football, struggling financially since the 1920s, became stronger in the late 1950s and early 1960s. Professional basketball became popular in the late 1950s. The success of the charismatic Arnold Palmer and the opening of thousands of public golf courses sent some ten million Americans onto the links on Saturdays and Sundays—and away from minor-league ballparks. Tennis and bowling became popular, too.

Transportation improvements also helped cripple the minors. Until the 1930s, for instance, minor-league teams in New Jersey had no trouble pulling in crowds, even though three major-league teams played just across the Hudson River in New York City. Then the George Washington Bridge and Holland and Lincoln tunnels were built, making it easy for New Jersey fans to cross the Hudson to see the big leagues.

The minors, reeling from all of this, were dealt knockout punches by their friends in the majors. The owners of major-league franchises, eager to make as much money as possible, began moving major-league teams into markets

that had proved successful for the minor leagues. The Boston Braves moved to Milwaukee in 1953, knocking out a long and successful minors team, the Brewers. In 1958 the Brooklyn Dodgers went to Los Angeles, killing the Angels and the Hollywood Stars. The New York Giants moved to San Francisco, booting out the Seals. Indeed, the relocation of the Dodgers and Giants to California nearly wrecked the entire Pacific Coast League, putting an end to whatever

TUCSON'S HY CORBETT FIELD WAS HOME TO MINOR-LEAGUE TEAMS FOR GENERATIONS. THE MAN WITH THE LARGE MEGAPHONE ANNOUNCED THE LINEUPS TO THE FANS AT THIS LATE-1950S GAME.

(OVERLEAF)
DISCH FIELD WAS HOME TO THE AUSTIN PIONEERS OF THE BIG STATE LEAGUE. TO MAKE CERTAIN EVERYONE KNEW WHO HAD BUILT IT, THE OWNER HAD GROUNDSKEEPERS CARVE HIS NAME IN THE OUTFIELD GRASS.

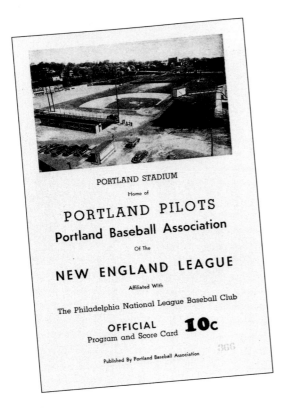

PORTLAND STADIUM
Home of

PORTLAND PILOTS
Portland Baseball Association
Of The

NEW ENGLAND LEAGUE

Affiliated With

The Philadelphia National League Baseball Club

OFFICIAL 10c
Program and Score Card

Published By Portland Baseball Association

AS YOU CAN SEE FROM THE PHOTO ON THE COVER OF THIS 1948 PROGRAM, THE PORTLAND PILOTS OF THE NEW ENGLAND LEAGUE PLAYED IN A RENOVATED HIGH SCHOOL FOOTBALL STADIUM.

dreams the league had for attaining major-league status. Major-league teams eventually moved into Atlanta, Oakland, Baltimore, Kansas City, Minneapolis, Montreal, San Diego, Seattle, and Toronto, and remain in these places today, putting the lid on minor-league play in each area. Minor-league teams tried hard to stay in business. Salaries were frozen. Teams looked for cheaper quarters—high school fields, with cheap leases, for instance, or local football fields, where an investment of just a few hundred dollars for fences could create a baseball diamond. Teams instituted "lucky number" systems, and fans won prizes—tickets to

upcoming games, car washes, spaghetti dinners, oil changes at local gas stations, defense bonds, shoes, hats, packs of Baby Ruth candy bars, appointments at local beauty parlors—if the lucky numbers were printed on their programs, tickets, or parking stubs. Ladies' Days came roaring back. The San Francisco Seals had Ladies' Days on Mondays and Fridays, and added a 1:30 P.M. game every Wednesday, billing it "Baseball for Businessmen" to entice workers to sneak out of the office.

Often, small towns and local entrepreneurs just didn't have the money to keep struggling teams going. Says Frank Michaloski, sixty-six, onetime member of a Poughkeepsie, New York, team that folded, along with the whole Colonial League, in the summer of 1950: "In Poughkeepsie, there were several local groups trying to save the team, but, local politics being what they are, they all started fighting among themselves. The result was that they couldn't put together a coalition to help the team and we lost it. When that team died, a piece of Poughkeepsie died."

By 1956 minor-league attendance had plummeted to just seventeen million. Thirty-one leagues and some 240 teams had gone out of business since 1949. The end was in sight.

"You'd sit wherever you wanted to see a game in the ballpark because nobody was there," says Clarence Smale,

EVERY MINOR-LEAGUE TEAM HAD ITS KNOTHOLE GANG, PROVIDING KIDS WITH FREE PASSES GOOD FOR MOST GAMES. KIDS IN LOUISVILLE, KENTUCKY, LINE UP HERE TO GET THEIR KNOTHOLE GANG PASS CARDS.

FRANK TORNAY, RIGHT, DALLAS THIRD BASEMAN, HOLDS A TEAMMATE BACK FROM TEMPTATION AS FINALISTS FOR THE MISS TEXAS LEAGUE BEAUTY TITLE ARRIVE AT BURNETT FIELD IN JUNE 1952. BEAUTY CONTESTS WERE A STAPLE OF MINOR-LEAGUE PROMOTIONS FROM COAST TO COAST.

now seventy-one, who followed the Reading Indians in the mid-1950s. "I think on their best night the Indians would draw about a thousand people. Usually it was just six hundred or seven hundred people. The high school football team would pull five times as many people."

Leagues brought in new teams. The Havana Sugar Kings approached the International League in 1953. The league was reluctant to take on the Sugar Kings, because teams like Toronto would have to make the long and

I MOVED TO ALABAMA FROM UP NORTH IN 1952 AND WENT TO MY FIRST BIRMINGHAM BARONS GAME THE FIRST MONTH I WAS THERE. I BOUGHT A BEER AT THE CONCESSION STAND AND STARTED TO WALK BACK TO THE SEAT. THIS BIG, BURLY, FRIGHTENING—AND I MEAN FRIGHTENING—COP STOPPED ME AND SAID "WHERE YOU GOING WITH THAT BEER?"

I TOLD HIM I WAS GOING TO MY SEAT. HE SAID THAT WAS NOT PERMITTED. PEOPLE DIDN'T DRINK BEER IN THE SEATS IN BIRMINGHAM. HE SAID I HAD TO DRINK IT AT THE CONCESSION STAND. THIS GUY WAS TEN FEET TALL AND HE HAD A GUN BIGGER THAN I WAS. WELL, I TOLD HIM THE BALLPARK HAD THE BEST BEER I EVER TASTED AND FINISHED THAT GLASS RIGHT THERE AT THE CONCESSION STAND, SMILING.
—HOWARD TRIPLETT, OF BIRMINGHAM, ALABAMA

FANS POINT PROUDLY TO AUSTIN'S AFFILIATION IN THE BIG STATE LEAGUE IN THE EARLY 1950S.

expensive flights back and forth to Cuba. Havana, determined to make a splash in American baseball—and eager to bring well-known teams into Cuba, then prosperous with millions of dollars of tourist money—agreed to compensate the league $60,000 for travel expenses. The Sugar Kings floundered for a few seasons but had a number of stars (pitcher Mike Cuellar was later a standout for the Baltimore Orioles) and in 1959 took the International League crown.

Politics doomed the Sugar Kings, though. Revolutionary Fidel Castro overthrew the government of Fulgencio Batista in the summer of 1959. On many breezy afternoons fans sitting in Gran Stadium could hear gunfire as the revolutionary army battled government troops for supremacy. The team was supported by Castro, a college

THE AUSTIN PIONEERS, LIKE SO MANY TEAMS, USED A CONVERTED SCHOOL BUS TO
TAKE PLAYERS TO AWAY GAMES. THIS ONE WAS TYPICAL. SOMETIMES NO DRIVER WAS
AVAILABLE AND A PLAYER WAS ASKED TO DRIVE (HE GOT FIVE DOLLARS A DAY EXTRA).

pitching star in Cuba himself, but by 1960 Castro was calling himself a communist. He began to seize U.S. property, and relations between the countries deteriorated rapidly. In midsummer the Sugar Kings moved out of Havana to Jersey City, New Jersey.

The owners of major-league teams, knowing that the fall of the minors would kill them (where would they get their players for nothing?), finally woke up in the spring of 1956 and created a $500,000 stabilization fund to save the minors. In 1959 hundreds of thousands of additional dollars were channeled to the minors in a player development fund. The final major-league "save the minors" plan went into effect in 1962—reclassification. The old system was changed to create new categories for different leagues: The top markets remained in class AAA, but the second tier was merged with the third tier as class AA. A new class A, combining classes C and D, was created. The majors also created rookie leagues for raw recruits and agreed to turn

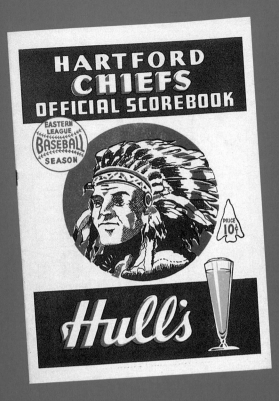

HARTFORD CHIEFS OFFICIAL SCOREBOOK

EASTERN LEAGUE BASEBALL SEASON

PRICE 10¢

Hull's

A Hartford Chiefs' scorecard from the 1947 season. Hull's, a local New England beer company, was a major sponsor of the ball club.

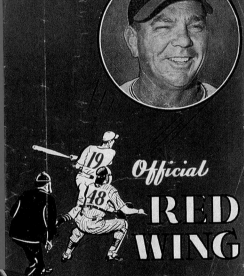

Price 10¢

Official **RED WING** SCORECARD

If the number on your parking stub matched the number in your Red Wings program, you won big prizes.

Programs for minor-league teams were just as stylish as those for the majors.

MINNEAPOLIS MILLERS 10¢

Charlie's café exceptionale

SCORE BOOK

BRIDGEPORT BEES OFFICIAL SCORE CARD

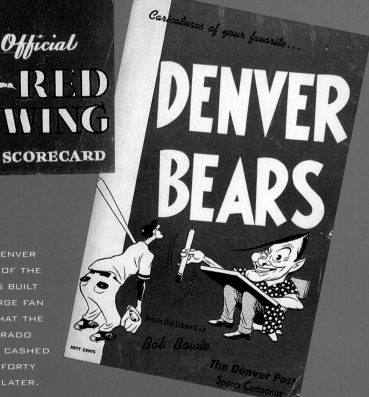

Caricatures of your favorite...

DENVER BEARS

FIFTY CENTS

From the inkwell of Bob Bowie

The Denver Post Sports Cartoonist

The Denver Bears of the 1950s built the large fan base that the Colorado Rockies cashed in on forty years later.

Many minor-league clubs sold "sketch books," similar to yearbooks.

The Chattanooga, Tennessee, Lookouts were the creation of Joe Engel, who during the Depression would feed as many as ten thousand people at the stadium on holidays.

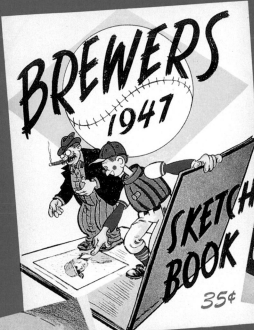

BREWERS 1947 SKETCH BOOK 35¢

Johnstown Uniontown Butler Vandergrift Oil City Youngstown Erie New Castle

1925 25th ANNIVERSARY 1949

MIDDLE ATLANTIC LEAGUE $1.00

The tiny Middle Atlantic League celebrated its twenty-fifth anniversary in 1949 with this colorful yearbook.

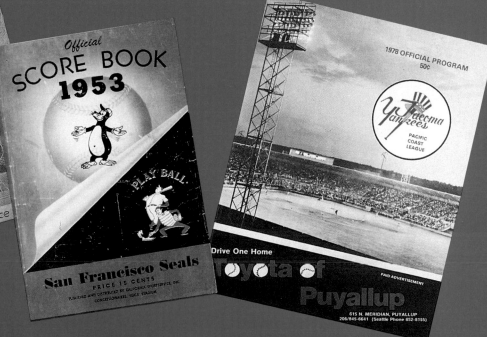

Your LOOKOUTS SINCE 1885.

1932 1939 1952 1982

price

by Wirt Gammon

Official SCORE BOOK 1953

PLAY BALL

San Francisco Seals

PRICE 15 CENTS

PUBLISHED AND DISTRIBUTED BY CALIFORNIA SPORTSERVICE, INC.
CONCESSIONAIRES, SEALS' STADIUM

1978 OFFICIAL PROGRAM 50¢

Tacoma Yankees

PACIFIC COAST LEAGUE

Drive One Home

Toyota of Puyallup

615 N. MERIDIAN, PUYALLUP
206/845-6641 (Seattle Phone 852-8155)

PAID ADVERTISEMENT

The Pacific Coast League always did everything right, including its programs.

BILLY PIERCE (LEFT) AND TED GRAY OF THE BUFFALO
BISONS. PIERCE WENT ON TO A LONG CAREER IN THE
MAJORS, WINNING 211 GAMES, MOST WITH THE CHICAGO
WHITE SOX. GRAY WENT ON TO A NINE-YEAR CAREER WITH
THE DETROIT TIGERS.

would in turn work harder to promote and run the club, helping ensure that the team would stay in business and the majors could keep their farm systems and development programs. Owners would profit from sales of tickets, souvenirs, food, and beverages. The new agreements also included a well-structured draft system in which the major-league team drafted each player, signed him to a major-league contract, and assigned him to one of their minor-league teams. The minor-league teams no longer "owned" any players.

Attendance bottomed out in 1963 and began to climb the next year, when minor-league attendance hit 9.9 million and there were eighteen leagues. The slide of the minors was halted. Attendance continued to rise slowly, but only to a scant twelve million by the middle of the 1970s, less than a third of what it was in the 1940s. Today the minors attract close to thirty million fans a year. Many of the newer teams folded, and so did older teams near major-league parks. The Newark Bears, so strong in the 1930s and 1940s, died after the 1949 season.

their financial agreements with the minors upside down, assuming most costs. In its simplest terms the complicated new arrangement meant that the parent club would now pay players' salaries and most of their expenses, but did not have to pay a fee when it brought a player up to the majors. Owners of the minor-league team, freed from the responsibility of bearing so much of the costs of their players,

> I USED TO GO TO THE BALLPARK IN LITTLE JAMESTOWN, NEW YORK, IN THE 1960S FOR THE NEW YORK–PENN LEAGUE GAMES. I THINK IF PEOPLE SAT ON EACH OTHER'S LAP IT HELD TWO THOUSAND. YOU WERE SO CLOSE TO THE PLAYERS YOU COULD HEAR THEM BREATHE. YOU'D HEAR THE SMACK OF THE BALL IN THE CATCHER'S MITT AND WHAT THE PITCHER YELLED AT THE UMP. IF THERE WAS A PERFECT PLACE TO SEE BASEBALL, IT WAS IN THAT LITTLE PARK IN JAMESTOWN.
>
> —PAUL KERN, OF POOLSVILLE, NEW YORK

Other older franchises managed to stay afloat financially, though, especially those far from major-league cities. Says Judge Burt Kolko, who worked at Red Wing Stadium in Rochester, New York, in the mid-1950s: "Rochester stayed alive in the fifties and sixties because there was no competition and because they had been there since the turn of the century and always had strong ties to the Cardinals, the parent club."

The minors were loaded with talented ballplayers in

JOHNNY BENCH PLAYED FOR BUFFALO, NEW YORK, BEFORE MOVING UP TO THE CINCINNATI REDS.

> IN MY FIRST YEARS IN THE MINORS IN 1954, FIVE OF US RENTED AN ATTIC FROM THIS COUPLE. THERE WERE THREE COTS AND ONE DOUBLE BUNK BED. OWENSBORO, KENTUCKY, IS A FURNACE IN SUMMER. IT WOULD BE OVER ONE HUNDRED DEGREES UP IN THAT ATTIC AND ALL WE HAD WAS THIS SMALL FAN THE OWNERS GAVE US. IT WAS SO HOT SOMETIMES THAT WE WRAPPED OURSELVES IN A SHEET AND SLEPT ON THE LAWN BEHIND THE HOUSE. YOU'D GET UP AT 5 A.M. BECAUSE THAT'S WHEN THE BIRDS GOT UP. THE BALLPARK WAS FOUR MILES FROM OUR HOUSE AND WE HAD TO WALK BOTH WAYS. FORTUNATELY, EXACTLY HALFWAY THERE WAS ONE OF THESE SMALL OLD ROADSIDE HIRES ROOT BEER STANDS, WHERE YOU GOT A BIG MUG OF ROOT BEER FOR A NICKEL.
>
> —TONY KUBEK, FORMER YANKEE SHORTSTOP AND NOW A BROADCASTER

the 1950s and 1960s. It was hard to move up from the minors, though, even with fewer teams. "The Yankees kept winning pennants and weren't about to change their lineup, so you had hundreds of guys in the Yankee system who were going nowhere," says pitcher Ralph Terry, who pitched for the Denver Bears before he finally did move up to the Yanks.

"Today a good ballplayer might do just a year or two in the minors and move up, but in the 1950s and early 1960s it was common practice for a team to keep a man in the minors five, six, seven years, no matter how good he was," says Brooks Robinson, who played several years for San Antonio and Vancouver before moving up to the Orioles and a sensational career.

> IN THE EARLY 1950S THE BOSTON RED SOX USED TO PLAY THE RICHMOND YANKEES ONCE EACH SUMMER IN A WEEKEND SERIES. WE ALL WENT TO SEE TED WILLIAMS, BUT HE NEVER PLAYED THE WHOLE GAME. I REMEMEBR ONE GAME WHEN HE CAME IN AS A PINCH HITTER IN THE NINTH AND HIT A FOUR-HUNDRED-FOOT HOMER. NEXT NIGHT, HE DIDN'T PLAY AGAIN. ONCE MORE, IN THE LAST INNING, THEY PUT HIM IN TO PINCH HIT AND HE HIT ANOTHER HOME RUN. WE WENT WILD. THE MOVIE PEOPLE COULDN'T SCRIPT SOMETHING LIKE THAT.
>
> —SAM COPPAGE, OF RICHMOND, VIRGINIA

Many talented minor leaguers went on to achieve fame in arenas other than baseball. In the summer of 1952 a young high school graduate trotted onto the outfield for Pittsburgh's farm club in Brunswick, Georgia. A highly touted teenage prospect, the center fielder hit a respectable .244 for eighty-one games but then was hit in the head with a pitch and hospitalized. During convalescence he decided to pursue a career in which people throw only insults, not baseballs. The player, Mario Cuomo, became the governor of New York.

Everybody talks to Cuomo about his minor-league days and over the years his one season has taken on mythic proportions. A study of that season shows that the governor of New York could handle pitchers as well as he later handled legislatures. From Pirate scout Ed McCarrick's report on Cuomo (far from the streets of New York City, Cuomo went as Matt, not Mario, that summer): "I think Cuomo has the tools to go all the way if the best can be brought out in him. He runs very well and should steal a lot of bases. . . . He has fine power and is very strong physically. . . . He is a fine hustler and competitor."

Cuomo, who still talks fondly of his playing days, was just one of many men who played minor-league baseball, never made it to the majors, and went on to do well in other fields. Quite a few were politicians. Scott Lucas looked like a superstar when he hit .462 in thirty-four games as a first baseman in the Illinois-Missouri League in 1913. His average dipped, but he still hit .283 for three seasons before changing careers and becoming a lawyer. Lucas eventually became a congressman from Illinois in 1934, was elected to the U.S. Senate in 1939, and served two years as majority leader. Young Frank Lausche had another spectacular debut, hitting a home run, triple, and single in his first game for Duluth, Minnesota, in the Northern League, in 1916. He tailed off, though, unable to hit curves, and hit .269 for the season. He hit just .155 for Lawrence, Massachusetts, in 1917, then went into the army and forgot baseball. Lausche later became mayor of Cleveland, Ohio (1941–45), governor of Ohio, and a U.S. senator.

A number of football players played baseball in the summer to make extra money, as Jim Thorpe had earlier. Beattie Feathers, an All American at the University of Tennessee, played seven years in the NFL and in the summer played baseball for minor-league teams in various southern leagues. He was as good with the bat as he was with the ball. Feathers hit .400 for three teams in eighty-four games in 1936, hit .300 in 1939, . 296 in 1942, and in his final season starred for Kingsport, Tennessee, in the Appalachian League, with a .343 average. Don Hutson, the All Pro receiver for the Green Bay Packers in the 1930s, hit .312 for Pine Bluff, Arkansas, in the Cotton States League in 1936 and .290 for two different teams in 1937. Sammy

Baugh, the Hall of Fame quarterback for the Washington Redskins in the 1930s and 1940s, played baseball for one summer, 1938, in Columbus, Ohio, and Rochester, New York. He hit just .200 and quit. Ken Strong and Kyle Rote, later stars with the New York Giants football team, also played minor-league ball. Art Rooney, owner of the Pittsburgh Steelers football team, played in the minors in 1922 and 1925, hitting a combined .363. John Elway, the quarterback for the Denver Broncos, hit .318 in his one season with the Oneonta, New York, minor-league team, before deciding for football. Basketball star Handy Andy Phillips,

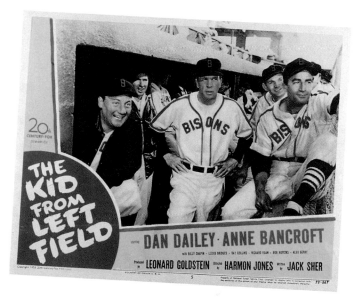

THE BUFFALO BISONS WERE THE SCREEN TEAM FOR THE FILM, "THE KID FROM LEFT FIELD."

THERE WERE TWO WAYS TO MAKE A FORTUNE AT ROCHESTER RED WING STADIUM AS A VENDOR IN 1956. ONE WAS THE TWI-NIGHT DOUBLEHEADER. SO THAT PEOPLE COULD COME FROM WORK AND STILL SEE TWO GAMES, THEY'D START AT FIVE AND ALWAYS MADE THE FIRST GAME JUST SEVEN INNINGS. BY THEN, PEOPLE WHO CAME FROM WORK WERE STARVED. IF I HAD THE HOT DOG ROUTE THAT NIGHT, I CLEANED UP. THE OTHER WAY WAS TO BE THE FIRST BEER VENDOR OUT IN FRONT OF THE BOX SEATS WHERE THE CORPORATE EXECUTIVES SAT. THOSE GUYS DRANK LIKE FISH. A FEW YEARS AGO I WAS BACK THERE AND THEY INTRODUCED ME AS A FORMER VENDOR WHO 'MADE GOOD' AND BROUGHT SOME OF THE TEENAGED VENDORS OVER TO HEAR SOME PEARLS OF WISDOM ON SUCCESS IN LIFE FROM THE JUDGE. I TOLD THEM TO WORK THE CORPORATE BOXES EARLY AND PUSH THE BEER.

—JUDGE BURTON S. KOLKO, OF WASHINGTON, D.C.

All American at Illinois and an NBA star in the 1950s, hit .281 in three minor-league seasons. Sweetwater Clifton, a star of the Harlem Globetrotters in the 1940s, hit .307 in the 1949 and 1950 seasons with teams in the Central, Can Am, and Eastern leagues.

Actor Kurt Russell played from 1971 to 1973 in the Northwest and Texas leagues and hit a very respectable .313. Randall Poffo, better known as Randy "Macho Man" Savage, world champion wrestler, got his athletic start playing the outfield in 1971 for Sarasota, Florida, in the Gulf Coast League, where he hit .286. He played four seasons in different leagues, hitting .254 (no, he did not play with his signature sequined sunglasses). Babe Dye, the NHL Hall of Famer, played in the minors from 1920 to 1926, hitting .313 lifetime. Country singer Jim Reeves played for Lynchburg, Tennessee, before switching to the microphone, as did

EVEN THOUGH THE MINORS WERE INTEGRATED IN 1946, MANY PLAYERS WENT TO PLAY ON MINOR-LEAGUE TEAMS IN CANADA, WHERE DISCRIMINATION WAS NOT AS BAD. LYMAN BOSTOCK PLAYED FOR THE WINNIPEG BUFFALOES IN THE EARLY 1950S.

The 1950s and 1960s also saw the end of the legendary player-manager job, created back in 1880 so the owners could save a salary. Some player-managers wound up owning their teams. Some wound up selling themselves to someone else. Frank Walker did just that in 1920. He was player-manager and owner of the Rocky Mount (North Carolina) Tar Heels and had a feeler from the Philadelphia A's. So Walker the owner got approval from Walker the manager to sell Walker the player for $5,000. The last player-manager was probably Earl Weaver, who later went on to be the highly successful manager of the Baltimore Orioles. Weaver, a talented hitter who once drove in 140 runs in one season in the minors, played second base. He misjudged a line drive one day and the ball hit him squarely in the chest, knocking him to the ground, where he lay motionless.

"I ran over to him and started shouting, 'Earl! Earl!'," remembers his first baseman that summer, Boog Powell. "After a minute or so, with great pain in his face, he opened his eyes slowly and looked up at me. 'I quit' he said. 'I'll never play again.'"

He didn't. He was helped off the field, returned the next day strictly as manager, and never played another inning.

Amazing records were set in the 1950s. Perhaps the most impressive was by young Ron Necciai, of Bristol, Virginia, in the Appalachian League. He struck out twenty-seven Welch, West Virginia, batters in a no-hitter on May 13, 1952, including four in one inning (following a base on a catcher's missed third-strike ball). He gave up three walks. The previous week, Necciai had struck out twenty batters on the Kingsport, Tennessee, team. The following week, again at Kingsport, he fanned twenty-four. He added nineteen more strikeouts a few days later against Pulaski, Virginia. In a stretch of thirty-six innings, he struck out ninety

Charley Pride. Gentleman Jim Corbett, heavyweight champion of the world in 1892, played because he knew he could make extra money as a gate attraction in minor-league games. Everybody wants to see the champ, reasoned Corbett, a decent ballplayer, so he had his manager book him as a "guest star" for different minor-league clubs, with Corbett pocketing 40 to 50 percent of the gate, much like a current rock star. He was worth the quarter to fifty cents fans were charged to see him play first base. Corbett earned some $17,000 for his thirty-five-game sojourn, or about twenty seasons' pay for a minor-league player.

batters. Pitcher Bill Bell attracted headlines just as big on May 26 of that year when he threw his second consecutive no-hitter, equaling the major-league double-no-hitter feat of Johnny Vander Meer (the first to do it anywhere was Clarence Wright, of Dayton, Ohio, in 1901).

The late 1950s and early 1960s were also the eras of the "bonus babies." The hot-shot high school and college players who the pro scouts were so certain would be stars began to hint that with their many skills they might play football or basketball instead of baseball. Since pro football and pro basketball were increasing in popularity, baseball owners were painted into a corner. To keep their top draft picks they began to offer bonuses as well as salaries. For the era, the bonuses were lavish. Most were between $35,000 and $50,000, but some went up to $100,000. Bob Bailey reportedly signed with the Pittsburgh Pirates for $200,000 in 1964. The majority of "bonus babies" did not become stars, however, and the bonus system fizzled after a few years. Of course, modern free-agents have since made salary packages of $400,000 and up commonplace.

Minor-league fans always had their eyes out for players who would make it big in the majors. People in Reading had the thrill of watching young Mike Schmidt, later a star with the Philadelphia Phillies, play there in the early 1970s.

"You could tell he'd be good the first time he stepped into the batter's box," says John Pasirba, sixty-four, of Ashland, Pennsylvania, who used to see Schmidt play in Reading. "He almost never struck out. Always hit the ball. He'd be able to see that ball the minute it left the pitcher's hand. Hit everything. Hit for average, hit for power, hit into the outfield alleys, drove in runners, hit clutch. Tremendous ballplayer. It was an event just to see him play."

The 1950s and 1960s were a time of superstars in the minors. Mickey Mantle, Carl Yastrzemski, Johnny Bench, Pete Rose, Orlando Cepeda, Willie McCovey, Nolan Ryan —perhaps in no era in history did so many players who went on to such success in the majors play minor-league ball. By the end of the 1970s, though, minor-league teams that used to pack fans into the outfield because the ballpark was sold out were letting people sit wherever they wanted in nearly empty stadiums. There did not seem to be much of a future, either, beyond the hundred or so teams the majors needed for their farms. Small city and small-town baseball was going the way of the horse and buggy, down the street and out of town. There wasn't much baseball on Main Street anymore.

> I WAS SCHEDULED TO PITCH, AND A GUY CALLED ME UP AT THE BOARDING HOUSE IN THE AFTERNOON AND IN THIS DEEP WHISPER SAID "NIGGER, IF YOU PITCH YOU'RE GOING TO GET SHOT RIGHT ON THE MOUND." I TOLD THE MANAGER WHAT HAPPENED AND THAT I WANTED TO PITCH. HE SAID GO AHEAD. I WAS NERVOUS. I WALKED TWO GUYS AND THEN I STARTED TO HEAR WHAT SOUNDED LIKE GUNSHOTS IN THE STANDS. IT WAS A FEW GUYS STOMPING ON EMPTY PAPER CUPS TO MAKE GUNSHOT SOUNDS. THEY LOOKED AT ME AND LAUGHED. THIS WAS THE SAME TIME BLACKS HAD DOGS SICCED ON THEM IN LITTLE ROCK. FOR THE FIRST TIME IN MY LIFE, I WAS A LITTLE SCARED. I LEFT THE GAME.
> —GRANT JACKSON, WHO PLAYED FOR THE ARKANSAS TRAVELERS IN THE EARLY 1960S AND IS NOW A COACH OF THE CHATTANOOGA LOOKOUTS

THE MINOR LEAGUES STRETCH FROM SEA TO SHINING SEA AND INTO
CANADA, TOO—A PROGRAM FROM OTTAWA, BATS FROM THE SOUTHERN
LEAGUE, AND A HAT FROM ALBUQUERQUE.

CHAPTER SIX

THE REVIVAL

The long, narrow Main Street of Frederick, Maryland, is lined with two- and three-story brick and stone buildings. Many of the stores have large white signs that swing from posts over the front doors. The town houses have short slate stoops with wrought-iron rails. Old, winding side streets, where generation after generation of families have lived, pour into Main Street, which leads out to a small cemetery and, behind it, the town's ballpark. Tucked into the foothills of the Catoctin Mountains, Frederick, one of the nation's oldest small towns, doesn't look much different today than it did in the Roaring Twenties, when it was part of the Blue Ridge League.

The town had a healthy baseball team in the old Blue Ridge League from 1915 to 1917 and from 1920 to 1930. The team shut down when the Depression hit, though, and it seemed like baseball had left Frederick for good. Then, in 1989 local entrepreneurs built one of the prettiest parks in the country and put a team back in Frederick. The Keys, of the Carolina League, are named after "Star-Spangled Banner" lyricist Francis Scott Key, who is buried in Frederick. The team sold out nearly every game in its first year and has been one of the most successful teams in the country ever since, drawing annual crowds of 300,000-plus, an example of how people can love again a baseball team they lost long ago.

The revival of baseball in Frederick is typical of the resurgence of interest in minor-league baseball that began sweeping across the country in the late 1970s and 1980s. There are several reasons for the renewed interest. Televised games, which once kept fans from baseballs parks, are now boosting attendance. The success of major-league baseball on television, aided by the advent of cable stations and superstations, has whetted the appetite of fans, who have been coming to ballparks to see the real thing. For many fans, minor-league ball is more fun than major-league play, which is sometimes accompanied by traffic jams, steep ticket prices, drinking, and inaccessible, superstar players. Three extraordinarily successful movies, *The Natural, Bull Durham,* and *Field of Dreams,* have combined nostalgia and baseball to tug at fans' hearts like no film since *The Pride of the Yankees.* These films seemed to turn on an emotional faucet that sent people teeming to ballparks—not only to Yankee Stadium and Candlestick Park but to small ballparks in small towns as well.

A family of four can still get free parking at a minor-league game, get great seats for three dollars a ticket, and buy hot dogs and sodas for a buck apiece. In a recessionary

FOLLOWING YOUR TEAM ON THE ROAD IS LIKE GOING ON VACATION. WE DRIVE ABOUT FIVE HOURS, STAY AT AN INEXPENSIVE HOTEL, EAT CHEAPLY, SEE TWO BALL GAMES, THEN DRIVE FIVE HOURS HOME. I CAN'T THINK OF A BETTER WAY TO SPEND A VACATION. WHAT WOULD YOU DO, SIT NEXT TO A POOL AT SOME RESORT? SAIL? FISH? PLAY GOLF? WHEN YOU COULD SEE A BALLGAME?

—DOREEN JOHANNES,
WHO FOLLOWS THE ROCHESTER (NEW YORK)
RED WINGS ON SIX TO EIGHT ROAD TRIPS
A YEAR WITH HER HUSBAND AND SON

era, these economics have helped the minors considerably. A new breed of minor-league owner has replaced the old guard, introducing new, streamlined marketing and promotion campaigns and convincing cities that it is in their economic interest to help keep teams and refurbish ballparks. The new owners have quickly cashed in on the boom in the memorabilia business, opening large souvenir shops.

Most of all, though, people are growing tired of life in the fast lane. A yearning for the slower, simpler times of years gone by has been rumbling through the land, from the Carolinas to the Rockies. The small-town atmosphere many people seem to want is to be found not in the huge, multimillion-dollar, cookie-cutter sports complexes of the majors, but in the tiny old bandbox stadiums of the minors, with their outfield walls painted over with advertising signs, real grass, wooden seats, badly painted ticket booths, and uneven fields.

Reading Municipal Stadium is a marvelous example of how the past is now galloping into the present. Craig

Stein, an accountant, bought the Reading Phillies in 1986 and was determined to take the stadium and its fans back to the past in this town where minor-league baseball has been played since the 1880s. He refurbished the front of the stadium with dark red brick and arches to make it look like a turn-of-the-century park, built a large picnic area for families with its own barbecue pit behind third base, hired a mascot, and began to pipe in music from the late 1940s to mid-1960s. As the fans leave the ballpark at the end of the game, the slow, haunting song "Goodnight, My Love" plays on the PA system.

"People are tired of the rat race. Life isn't what it used to be," says Stein, dressed in neatly pressed tan slacks and a dark sports shirt as he smiled and greeted dozens of fans walking into the ballpark. "When I was a kid in the fifties, life was simpler. It was better. People didn't have to commute two hours to work. Everybody didn't get divorced. You could walk the city streets at night. Beer wasn't four bucks a glass. I want people to come to my ballpark and turn back the clock to the forties and fifties and sixties and, regardless of age, close their eyes and be kids again."

The minor-league associations have been making an effort to bring back the old glory, too. The American Association and International League champs have begun to play each other in a championship series at the end of the year, reviving the defunct Junior World Series. The Pacific Coast League, a AAA league, has expanded. The 1988 U.S. Olympic baseball team, led by Jim Abbott, won the gold medal and went on a national tour, playing in dozens of minor-league ballparks.

The minors have grown steadily since the early 1960s, when they wallowed in baseball's low tide. Today there are more than two hundred minor league teams in towns and

DON MATTINGLY MADE HIS DEBUT WITH NASHVILLE AND THEN STARRED AT COLUMBUS, OHIO, BEFORE MOVING UP TO THE YANKEES AND STARDOM.

DOC GOODEN CAME UP WITH TIDEWATER, VIRGINIA.

BENITO SANTIAGO MADE HIS MARK WITH THE LAS VEGAS STARS.

T O ME, THE FUN IS SEEING GREAT PLAYERS BEFORE THEY GET TO THE MAJORS, BEFORE ANYBODY KNOWS THEM. THEN, TWO OR THREE YEARS LATER, WHEN THE PLAYERS ARE SUPERSTARS, YOU CAN SHOW YOUR FRIENDS PICTURES OF YOU WITH THEM, ALL THE THINGS THEY AUTOGRAPHED FOR YOU, AND HOW YOU WERE FRIENDS WITH THEM.

—DUSTIN HALUSKA, 13, OF READING, PENNSYLVANIA

MICHAEL TUCKER, WHO PLAYED ON THE 1992 OLYMPIC
TEAM, SIGNED THIS BAT LAST SUMMER, WHEN HE PLAYED
FOR THE MEMPHIS CHICKS. THE PROGRAM CELEBRATES
THE RENOVATION OF TIM MCCARVER STADIUM IN MEMPHIS.

JOE BUZAS, A FINE PLAYER HIMSELF, WAS ONE
OF THE KEY FIGURES IN THE 1980S REVIVAL
OF THE MINORS.

TICKET STUBS TELL PART OF THE REASON THE
MINORS ARE BOUNCING BACK: TICKETS COST A
FRACTION OF WHAT THEY DO IN THE MAJORS.

E VERYBODY WATCHES THEIR
BUDGET THESE DAYS. FOR US,
TAKING THE KIDS TO THE BALLPARK IS
CHEAP AND A LOT OF FUN. THERE'S
SOMETHING SLOW AND LAZY ABOUT
IT. YOU DON'T TALK TO YOUR KIDS
WHEN YOU GO TO THE MOVIES OR THE
AMUSEMENT PARK. AT THE BALL GAME
YOU CAN JUST SIT THERE AND TALK
AND WATCH AND TALK. IT'S NICE.

—SUZANNE BAKER,
OF FRANKLIN, TENNESSEE

cities that range in size from tiny Hickory, North Carolina, to bustling Las Vegas, Nevada. There are fewer leagues than in the glory days of the minors in the 1930s and 1940s, but the leagues are stronger and more stable. The 1963 agreements with the major-league teams, updated over the years, permit minor-league teams to operate relatively independently of their parent club. The parent pays the salaries, and the minor-league club carries the burden of operating the ballpark, promoting games, paying park personnel, and paying some travel expenses. Major-league teams own all the minor-league clubs except those in the small, independent Northern League. Most major-league teams support six or seven minor-league teams and promote players up through their ranks. Some players move up through three levels of play in three years; others do it in a single summer.

There are many who go up to the big leagues for the "cup of coffee," a stay so brief it lasts no longer than the time it takes to wolf down a mug of coffee. Tack Wilson, a fourteen-year minor-league veteran and now a hitting instructor for the Atlanta Braves farm system at a minor-league park, says, " I was up with the Twins for one week in 1983. I got into one game and, on a single in front of me, I overthrew the cut-off man. Two days later I was sent packing and told I couldn't play the field."

Wilson's is a familiar story. Greg Legg of the Scranton, Pennsylvania, Red Barons has been playing baseball for twelve years and gone to the majors for two short stays. I'm better now at thirty four than I was at twenty four," he says. "I'm not too old. I'll get to the majors and I'll stick. It's going to be my last hurrah. . . ."

It's even more frustrating for those who skyrocket out of the minors to the majors for a season or two, stay in the big leagues for several years, then get sent down. Glenn

Sutko was one of them. After a single season in the minors he moved up as the catcher for the Cincinnati Reds, where he played decently for two years but was sent down. Refusing to be washed out of the game at age twenty five, Sutko retrained himself and became a pitcher for the Winston-Salem, North Carolina, Spirits. He's hoping to make it back to the Reds as a hurler. "I'm going to do it. If I wasn't good enough as a catcher, I'll be good enough as a pitcher. If the Reds don't want me anymore, I'll hook on with someone else. I'm gonna make it back."

Although most players say they should go the majors after a year or two, some players believe being held back in the minors actually helped them. One is Wade Boggs, the longtime Red Sox star and current Yankee, who spent six long years in the minors before getting the call. "I went into baseball at age seventeen. I was immature and I knew it. I needed six seasons to learn the game, learn what I was good at and not so good at. I learned to read pitchers, to hit to different fields. When I did move up to the majors, I was ready. I was better off being held back."

No matter how many years they've played, all minor leaguers want to wind up just like Jeffrey Hammonds,

---

IN 1983 I UNDERWENT TRIPLE BYPASS SURGERY AND WASN'T GIVEN MUCH TIME. THE DOCTOR SAID WHATEVER TIME I HAD LEFT SHOULD BE SPENT DOING ONLY THINGS THAT GAVE MY PLEASURE. I QUIT WORKING AND BOUGHT SEASON TICKETS TO THE REDBIRDS. I HAVEN'T MISSED A GAME SINCE, AND I'M HEALTHIER NOW THAN I WAS THEN.

—BILL METZGER, OF LOUISVILLE, KENTUCKY

twenty-four, the number one pick of the Orioles. Hammonds played for the 1992 Olympic team. Then, one morning in late June of 1993, his phone rang. It was Hall of Fame slugger and Baltimore Orioles exec Frank Robinson.

It was time to go to the big leagues. Hammonds was so excited he missed his plane. After a speedy cab ride from the airport, he didn't get to Orioles stadium in Baltimore until the end of the first inning. No sooner did he sit down in the dugout than manager Johnny Oates walked over to him and told him he was the designated hitter that night.

Hammonds stepped into the batter's box in the third inning to a round of polite applause from the fans in the jammed to capacity stadium as the scoreboard announced it was his first major-league at bat. On the second pitch, a high fastball, he ripped a clean single to the left and the stadium erupted in rolling thunder. Forty-eight thousand people stood and cheered the young rookie collecting his first major-league hit in his first at bat. "It was just like I thought it would be when I was a boy," said Hammonds after the game, his locker surrounded by reporters. "Just like in my dreams."

THE REVIVAL OF THE MINORS WAS LED BY THE BUFFALO BISONS. THE TEAM BUILT NINETEEN-THOUSAND-SEAT PILOT FIELD, ONE OF THE COUNTRY'S PRETTIEST BALLPARKS, IN 1989.

OPPOSITE: PILOT FIELD MAY BE THE JEWEL OF MODERN MINOR-LEAGUE PARKS, BUT THE BALLPARK IN MIDLAND, TEXAS, IS MORE TYPICAL. THE STADIUM, WHICH SEATS FIVE THOUSAND, IS A SINGLE-TIER BALLPARK WITH MINIMAL ROOF AND A SMALL PRESS BOX STUCK ON THE TOP.

IT TAKES ME OVER AN HOUR TO DRIVE TO BALTIMORE TO SEE THE ORIOLES. IT TAKES THREE MINUTES TO DRIVE DOWN MAIN STREET TO SEE THE KEYS. THAT'S WHY THE MINORS ARE SO SUCCESSFUL—THEY ARE YOUR TOWN'S TEAM.

—PAUL PIERCE, OF FREDERICK, MARYLAND

and newspaper attention was riveted on the longest game in baseball history, a thirty-three-inning, eight-hour game between the Pawtucket (Rhode Island) Red Sox and Rochester (New York) Red Wings. The umpires called the game

MEMPHIS CHICKS

Jim Keras NISSAN
$210,000
CAR GIVEAWAY
A WINNER EVERY HOME GAME!
WREC **ROCK 103**
600 AM • MEMPHIS · MEMPHIS' CLASSIC

This is Your
Lucky Number
For Tonight's
**Drawing To Be
Held In The
Eighth Inning**
(You MUST have this to win)

119640

No Purchase Necessary. Must be over 18 years of age. Must be present to win. Free Chicks tickets are available at Jim Keras Nissan, 2110 Covington Pike, Memphis, TN 38128. Winner will be chosen by random drawing during the eighth inning of each home game during the 1993 season. Winner is responsible for all applicable taxes, as well as car tags and inspection sticker. Cars are "as is" without warranty. Cars are previously owned, of various makes, models and year—no guarantee expressed or implied as to the actual retail value of vehicles. One winner per household.

ONE OF MANY MODERN GIVEAWAYS, WHICH HELP DRAW LARGE CROWDS TO MINOR-LEAGUE BALLPARKS.

SEVERAL MINOR LEAGUES STILL HAVE THEIR OWN MAGAZINES.

The twenty-one minor leagues are broken down by the caliber of play and size of the home city. The largest cities host the Triple A leagues: the International, Pacific Coast, and Mexican leagues, and the American Association. The Double A leagues are the Eastern, Southern, and Texas leagues. Single A circuits are the Carolina, Florida State, Midwest, and South Atlantic leagues. Short Season Single A circuits (playing a seventy-game season) are the New York–Penn League and the Northwest League. Rookie leagues, the lowest level, are the Appalachian, Pioneer, Arizona, Gulf Coast, Northern, Dominica Summer, and Arizona Fall leagues.

The minors, which haven't been in the news for decades, have been making headlines again. In 1981 television

THE LYNX BROUGHT BASEBALL TO OTTAWA FOR THE FIRST TIME AND PULLED RECORD CROWDS.

SCHEDULES FROM THE RICHMOND, VIRGINIA, BRAVES AND
THE GREENVILLE, SOUTH CAROLINA, BRAVES.

A SOUVENIR
PROGRAM
AND BRACE
OF TICKETS
FROM MIKE
SCHMIDT DAY
IN READING,
PENNSYLVANIA.

at 4 A.M. on the second day because everyone was worn out and there were no pitchers left. The game was concluded two months later. Media attention came the way of the minors again in 1986, when football star Bo Jackson was sent to the Memphis Chicks as a warm up for his Chicago White Sox debut.

The new revival of interest in the minors has caused attendance to climb. Twelve million. Fourteen million. Sixteen million. Twenty million. Twenty-eight million in 1993. After the release of the movie *Bull Durham* there was such a request for Bulls memorabilia from around the United States and abroad that the team had to set up a direct-mail office. Potential owners who had not wanted to risk their money in the climate of the 1960s and 1970s started to buy franchises. The majors helped, too, by ordering minor-league ballparks they owned to be refurbished. (Players and scouts had been complaining that players didn't have a fair chance to show what they could do in run-down ball-parks. New rules were set, requiring minor-league parks to meet certain standards. Some had to build brand-new stadiums to meet the requirements and keep their teams.)

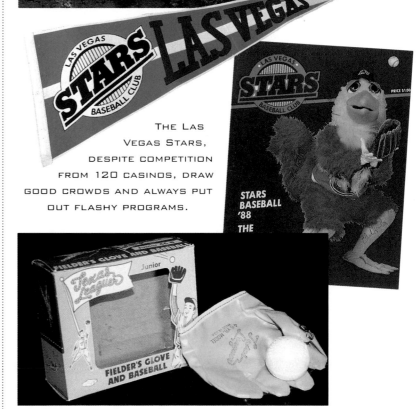

THE LAS
VEGAS STARS,
DESPITE COMPETITION
FROM 120 CASINOS, DRAW
GOOD CROWDS AND ALWAYS PUT
OUT FLASHY PROGRAMS.

TEXAS LEAGUE KIDS' GLOVES FROM THE MID-1950S.

MAX PATKIN, THE "CLOWN PRINCE OF BASEBALL," DOES HIS GOOFY ROUTINES AT MORE THAN 150 BALLPARKS EACH SUMMER AND IS A FAN FAVORITE.

Celebrities bought teams. Counties bought teams. Lackawanna County, in the coal country of Pennsylvania, which had so much wonderful baseball in the first half of the century, lost its last minor-league team in the 1950s, when the mines started to shut down. In 1992, buoyed by public support, the county built Lackawanna Stadium, a beautiful, state-of-the-art, ten-thousand-seat facility set softly into a valley, where deer and bears roam the cliffs behind the outfield fences. Local politicians had estimated that as many as 300,000 people would attend games in the

first year alone, a wildly optimistic prediction that baseball people scoffed at. The first summer more than 500,000 fans showed up to watch the Scranton–Wilkes Barre Red Barons play there.

Louisville, Kentucky, where professional baseball had been played since 1876, lost its team in 1972. Ten years later a new Louisville team, the Redbirds, began drawing all-time record crowds of more than one million fans per summer. Minor-league ball returned to Nashville in 1982, twenty years after it left, and has done well. Prince William County, in Virginia, has recently built a new park for its team, the Cannons, in the Carolina League. In 1992, after forty years, minor-league baseball returned to Ottawa, Ontario, and the team, the Lynx, has been drawing record crowds. After forty years, baseball returned to Wilmington, Delaware, in 1993, doing near-capacity business. New Haven, Connecticut, got a new minor-league team, the Ravens, in April 1994. New Jersey has two new teams, the first minor-league teams in the state in thirty-five years. Miles Wolff, publisher of *Baseball America,* a weekly newspaper, just revived the Northern League, which flourished in the Midwest in the 1940s and 1950s, as an independent circuit with no major-league subsidy. The league's owners were confident that a well-organized league, with salary caps to keep down costs, would permit local teams to make money, play good baseball, and provide a competitive game to showcase the talents of players. League officials promoted the league heavily, worked with local merchants on advertising and ticket campaigns, and invited major-league scouts to check out the players. The league began in 1993 with teams in Duluth, Saint Paul, and Rochester, Minnesota; Sioux Falls, South Dakota; Sioux City, Iowa; and Thunder Bay, Ontario. All of the opening day games sold out.

Says Wolff, the league's organizer, who goes to the ballpark regularly with his wife and two children:

America has become a country where for entertainment and community bonding everybody goes shopping at a mall. There was a time when people walked the village green at night, greeting each other. There was a time when people spent hours on the streets where they lived, catching up on local news. . . . That's disappearing. Minor-league ballparks restore that. Everybody, young, old, black, white, town, gown, rich and poor, can go to their town's ballpark and socialize. They come an hour early, have dinner together, visit friends, borrow $5, return a tape. The minor-league ballpark has become the new village green for small towns. A ballpark makes people feel comfortable and good about things.

Tab Brockman, marketing director for the Louisville Redbirds, says, "If you run your team properly you have little competition in most minor-league towns. The big-city baseball teams compete with pro football, basketball, and hockey, but we don't. Minor league baseball is in most small cities, so if you do the job, you'll have a market to pull from."

Al Mangum, the general manager of the Durham Bulls, thinks the minors have succeeded because they have become businesses. "Teams now are run like corporations, with streamlined accounting, promotions, and heavy duty marketing. In the sixties, teams were run by one or two guys who opened the gate and hoped somebody would show up," he says.

Mangum talked in his trailer office at the Bulls ballpark, watching the radar screen on the Weather Channel to see if that night's game would be rained out (it was not and the Bulls won). Outside his window not one, not two, but three different mascots cavorted in the stands (the

> **S**OMETIMES GUYS FIND OUT THE CAROLINA CHICKEN IS REALLY A WOMAN. THEN I GET HANDLED A LOT. I DON'T UNDERSTAND. LIKE I'M REALLY GOING TO GO FOR A GUY WHO GETS OFF ON A CHICKEN. . . .
> —PATTI AUEN, OF RALEIGH, NORTH CAROLINA, THE "CAROLINA CHICKEN"

YES, IT IS A REAL MONKEY. THIS SIMIAN BASEBALL FAN WAS THE MIDLAND ANGELS MASCOT IN 1977. NO ONE KNOWS IF HE WAS CARDED FOR BEER.

DARREN WINSTON, OF THE HARRISBURG SENATORS,
EASTERN LEAGUE, OBLIGES AN AUTOGRAPH HOUND.

Durham Bull, the Carolina Chicken, and Tony the Tiger).
Sometimes the Bulls offer sodas and hot dogs at twenty-
five cents or bring in Bulls players from years gone by to
sign autographs.

The minors specialize in promotion and hoopla. They
give away cups, hats, tee-shirts, baseball card sets, bags, seat
cushions, player photos, batting helmets, tumblers, sunglasses, autographed balls, bats, desk folders, watches, pins,
pennants, wristbands, team photos, and jackets. They sponsor home-run derbies with retired stars, fireworks displays,
human bowling-ball contests, costume contests, soap opera
stars, softball games, and concerts with the Beach Boys and
other groups. And everybody, but everybody, hires Max
Patkin, the buffoonish clown prince of baseball, to entertain
fans at least once a season with his sight gags, pantomime,
acrobatics, and outlandish uniforms.

"The promotions make the ballpark a fun place to go
and that builds family business," says Larry Schmittou, who

has owned several minor league teams and now runs the
Nashville (Tennessee) Sounds and Huntsville (Alabama)
Stars. "The promotions, and the marketing of the pro-
motions, have helped the minors more than anything else.
You have to get the people to come out for the fun of it."

People who come to the minors for the first time go
home feeling as if they've found buried treasure. That's
what happened to Kevin Sholley, of Meyerstown, Pennsylvania, who took his son to a Reading game in early April
1992 and wound up going to sixty more games that season.
In 1993 Sholley and his twelve-year-old boy, Jason, went to
another sixty games and even made road trips with the
team. "It's like a carnival, really. It's been the discovery of
our lives," said Sholley.

Longtime major-league fans who visit a minor-league
ballpark often switch allegiances. "In 1992, my son and I
saw fifty Yankee games," says Jack Wayser of Scotch Plains,
New Jersey. "For a diversion, we went to a minor-league
game and just fell in love. It's very casual and festive and
you see good, hard baseball. Most important to me, it's safe
for the kids. I sit here and watch the game and my kid
wanders around the stadium and I don't worry. In New
York, I would never let him wander two feet from me."

Minor-league ballplayers are more accessible to fans
than their colleagues in the majors. "Minor-league players
enjoy talking to fans," says Dave Bush, a fan of Pennsylvania's Scranton–Wilkes Barre Red Barons, as he leans
over the railing to talk to two players. "In the majors, none
of the players can be bothered anymore. They must get a
disease up there or something."

In many ways, the contemporary minors are moving
back in time closer to the minors of old. Because the
money in the majors is so good now ($100,000 minimum

salary and close to $1 million a year for many), many minor-league stars are hanging on and playing for ten or more years, as they did back in the 1920s, hoping to move up. Many of the new stadiums, such as the one the Durham Bulls moved into in 1994, are designed to look like the old ones. Other parks, such as McCarver Stadium in Memphis, are being renovated in old style, with grandstand roofs held up with pillars and flags flying from the tops. Many teams have turn-back-the-clock night, at which players from both teams wear uniforms of a bygone season, programs of that year are duplicated, and the overall decor and spirit of the park reflect that era. The knothole gang has returned at many ballparks, as have old timers games.

Even town ball, so popular years ago, is back in the minors. Each summer, the towns of Cape Cod, Massachu-setts, fielding teams of current college stars, battle each other at high school fields and in town parks. Nicknames are back, thanks to Motorboat Jones, Bubba Smith, Skeeter Barnes, and others. New teams are taking the names of now-defunct teams that once played in the same towns, such as the Wilmington Blue Rocks and Scranton–Wilkes Barre Red Barons. Today's outfield fences are covered with ads, just as they were in 1935. Inexorably, as the years go by, the minor leagues are borne back into the past. In small city after small city, small town after small town, crowds of happy people, many with their tired kids clutching their hands, leave the ballparks and head home, full of baseball and their community. Many feel tugged into the past, like those in Reading, who leave the ballpark under high old brick arches as the music of "Goodnight, My Love" drifts over the city.

READING (PENNSYLVANIA) MUNICIPAL WAS BUILT IN 1951, BUT RECENTLY UNDERWENT A RENOVATION THAT INCLUDED TURN-OF-THE-CENTURY-STYLE BRICK ARCHES. IT'S ONE OF THE COUNTRY'S MOST CHARMING OLD BALLPARKS.

MICHAEL JORDAN: THE KING OF BASKETBALL RETIRED FROM
THE COURT TO JOIN THE WHITE SOX FARM SYSTEM—AND BECOME
THE MOST CELEBRATED MINOR LEAGUER EVER.

WHERE THE TEAMS ARE

ALABAMA

Birmingham	Barons	Southern League	Chicago White Sox
Huntsville	Stars	Southern League	Kansas City Athletics
Mobile	Bay Sharks	Texas-Louisiana League	Independent

ARIZONA

| Phoenix | Firebirds | Pacific Coast League | San Francisco Giants |
| Tucson | Toros | Pacific Coast League | Houston Astros |

ARKANSAS

| Little Rock | Travelers | Texas League | St. Louis Cardinals |

CALIFORNIA

Adelanto	High Desert Mavericks	California League	Florida Marlins
Bakersfield	Dodgers	California League	Los Angeles Dodgers
Lake Elsinor	Storm	California League	California Angels
Modesto	Athletics	California League	Oakland Athletics
Rancho Cucamonga	Quakes	California League	San Diego Padres
Riverside	Pilots	California League	Seattle Mariners
San Bernardino	The Spirit	California League	Independent
San Jose	Giants	California League	San Francisco Giants
Stockton	Ports	California League	Milwaukee Brewers
Visalia	Central Valley Rockies	California League	Colorado Rockies

COLORADO

| Colorado Springs | Sky Sox | Pacific Coast League | Colorado Rockies |

CONNECTICUT

| New Britain | Red Sox | Eastern League | Boston Red Sox |
| New Haven | Ravens | Eastern League | Colorado Rockies |

DELAWARE

| Wilmington | Blue Rocks | Carolina League | Kansas City Royals |

FLORIDA

Charlotte	Rangers	Florida State League	Texas Rangers
Clearwater	Phillies	Florida State League	Philadelphia Phillies
Daytona	Cubs	Florida State League	Chicago Cubs
Dunedin	Blue Jays	Florida State League	Toronto Blue Jays
Fort Myers	Miracle	Florida State League	Minnesota Twins
Jacksonville	Suns	Southern League	Seattle Mariners
Lakeland	Tigers	Florida State League	Detroit Tigers
Melbourne	Marlins	Florida State League	Florida Marlins
Orlando	Cubs	Southern League	Chicago Cubs
Osceola	Astros	Florida State League	Houston Astros
Tampa	Yankees	Florida State League	New York Yankees
St. Lucie	Mets	Florida State League	New York Mets
St. Petersburg	Cardinals	Florida State League	St. Louis Cardinals
Sarasota	Red Sox	Florida State League	Boston Red Sox
Vero Beach	Dodgers	Florida State League	Los Angeles Dodgers
West Palm Beach	Expos	Florida State League	Montreal Expos

GEORGIA

Albany	Polecats	South Atlantic League	Baltimore Orioles
Augusta	Pirates	South Atlantic League	Pittsburgh Pirates
Columbus	Redstixx	South Atlantic League	Cleveland Indians
Macon	Braves	South Atlantic League	Atlanta Braves
Savannah	Cardinals	South Atlantic League	St. Louis Cardinals

IDAHO

| Boise | Hawks | Northwest League | California Angels |
| Idaho Falls | Braves | Pioneer League | Atlanta Braves |

ILLINOIS

Geneva	Kane County Cougars	Midwest League	Florida Marlins
Peoria	Chiefs	Midwest League	Chicago Cubs
Rockford	Royals	Midwest League	Montreal Expos

INDIANA

Ft. Wayne	Wizards	Midwest League	Minnesota Twins
Indianapolis	Indians	American Association	Cincinnati Reds
South Bend	White Sox	Midwest League	Chicago White Sox

IOWA

Burlington	B's	Midwest League	Montreal Expos
Cedar Rapids	Kernels	Midwest League	California Angels
Clinton	Giants	Midwest League	San Francisco Giants
Davenport	Quad City River Bandits	Midwest League	Houston Astros
Des Moines	Iowa Cubs	American Association	Chicago Cubs
Sioux City	Explorers	Northern League	Independent
Waterloo	Diamonds	Midwest League	San Diego Padres

KANSAS

Wichita	Wranglers	Texas League	San Diego Padres

KENTUCKY

Louisville	Redbirds	American Association	St. Louis Cardinals

LOUISIANA

Alexandria	Aces	Texas-Louisiana League	Independent
New Orleans	Zephyrs	American Association	Milwaukee Brewers
Shreveport	Captains	Texas League	San Francisco Giants

MAINE

Portland	Sea Dogs	Eastern League	Florida Marlins

MARYLAND

Bowie	Baysox	Eastern League	Baltimore Orioles
Frederick	Keys	Carolina League	Baltimore Orioles
Hagerstown	Suns	South Atlantic League	Toronto Blue Jays

MASSACHUSETTS

Pittsfield	Mets	New York-Penn League	New York Mets

MICHIGAN

Grand Rapids	West Michigan White Caps	Midwest League	Oakland Athletics

MINNESOTA

Duluth-Superior	Dukes	Northern League	Independent
St. Paul	Saints	Northern League	Independent

MISSISSIPPI

Jackson	Generals	Texas League	Houston Astros

MONTANA

Billings	Mustangs	Pioneer League	Cincinnati Reds
Butte	Copper Kings	Pioneer League	Independent
Great Falls	Dodgers	Pioneer League	Los Angeles Dodgers
Helena	Brewers	Pioneer League	Milwaukee Brewers

NEBRASKA

Omaha	Royals	American Association	Kansas City Royals

NEVADA

Las Vegas	Stars	Pacific Coast League	San Diego Padres

NEW JERSEY

Trenton	Thunder	Eastern League	Detroit Tigers
Sussex	New Jersey Cardinals	New York-Penn League	St. Louis Cardinals

NEW MEXICO

Albuquerque	Dukes	Pacific Coast League	Los Angeles Dodgers

NEW YORK

Albany-Colonie	Yankees	Eastern League	New York Yankees
Auburn	Astros	New York-Penn League	Houston Astros
Batavia	Clippers	New York-Penn League	Philadelphia Phillies
Binghamton	Mets	Eastern League	New York Mets
Buffalo	Bisons	American Association	Pittsburgh Pirates
Elmira	Pioneers	New York-Penn League	Florida Marlins
Fishkill	Hudson Valley Sailors	New York-Penn League	Texas Rangers
Jamestown	Tigers	New York-Penn League	Detroit Tigers
Oneonta	Yankees	New York-Penn League	New York Yankees
Rochester	Red Wings	International League	Baltimore Orioles
Syracuse	Chiefs	International League	Toronto Blue Jays
Utica	Blue Sox	New York-Penn League	Boston Red Sox
Watertown	Indians	New York-Penn League	Cleveland Indians

NORTH CAROLINA

Asheville	Tourists	South Atlantic League	Houston Astros
Burlington	Indians	Appalachian League	Cleveland Indians
Durham	Bulls	Carolina League	Atlanta Braves
Fayetteville	Generals	South Atlantic League	Detroit Tigers
Greensboro	Hornets	South Atlantic League	New York Yankees
Hickory	Crawdads	South Atlantic League	Chicago White Sox
Kinston	Indians	Carolina League	Cleveland Indians
Winston-Salem	Spirits	Carolina League	Cincinnati Reds
Zebulon	Carolina Mudcats	Southern League	Pittsburgh Pirates

OHIO

Canton-Akron	Indians	Eastern League	Cleveland Indians
Columbus	Clippers	International League	New York Yankees
Toledo	Mud Hens	International League	Detroit Tigers

OKLAHOMA

Oklahoma City	89ers	American Association	Texas Rangers
Tulsa	Drillers	Texas League	Texas Rangers

OREGON

Bend	Rockies	Northwest League	Colorado Rockies
Eugene	Emeralds	Northwest League	Kansas City Royals
Medford	Southern Oregon Athletics	Northwest League	Oakland Athletics

PENNSYLVANIA

Harrisburg	Senators	Eastern League	Montreal Expos
Reading	Phillies	Eastern League	Philadelphia Phillies
Scranton	Scranton-Wilkes Barre Red Barons	International League	Philadelphia Phillies
Williamsport	Cubs	New York-Penn League	Chicago Cubs

RHODE ISLAND

Pawtucket	Red Sox	International League	Boston Red Sox

SOUTH CAROLINA

Charleston	Rainbows	South Atlantic League	Texas Rangers
Charlotte	Knights	International League	Cleveland Indians
Columbia	Capital City Bombers	South Atlantic League	New York Mets
Greenville	Braves	Southern League	Atlanta Braves
Spartanburg	Phillies	South Atlantic League	Philadelphia Phillies

SOUTH DAKOTA

Sioux Falls	Canaries	Northern League	Independent

TENNESSEE

Chattanooga	Lookouts	Southern League	Cincinnati Reds
Elizabethton	Twins	Appalachian League	Minnesota Twins
Johnson City	Cardinals	Appalachian League	St. Louis Cardinals
Kingsport	Mets	Appalachian League	New York Mets
Knoxville	Smokies	Southern League	Toronto Blue Jays
Memphis	Chicks	Southern League	Kansas City Royals
Nashville	Sounds	American Association	Chicago White Sox

TEXAS

Amarillo	Dillas	Texas-Louisiana League	Independent
Beaumont	Bullfrogs	Texas-Louisiana League	Independent
Corpus Christi	Barracudas	Texas-Louisiana League	Independent
El Paso	Diablos	Texas League	Milwaukee Brewers
Midland	Angels	Texas League	California Angels
Rio Grande Valley	White Wings	Texas-Louisiana League	Independent
San Antonio	Missions	Texas League	Los Angeles Dodgers
San Antonio	Tejanos	Texas-Louisiana League	Independent
Tyler	Wildcats	Texas-Louisiana League	Independent

UTAH

Ogden	Raptors	Pioneer League	Independent
Salt Lake City	Buzz	Pacific Coast League	Minnesota Twins

VERMONT

Winooski	Expos	New York-Penn League	Montreal Expos

VIRGINIA

Bristol	Tigers	Appalachian League	Detroit Tigers
Danville	Braves	Appalachian League	Atlanta Braves
Lynchburg	Red Sox	Carolina League	Boston Red Sox
Martinsville	Phillies	Appalachian League	Philadelphia Phillies
Norfolk	Tides	International League	New York Mets
Prince William	Cannons	Carolina League	New York Yankees
Richmond	Braves	International League	Atlanta Braves
Salem	Buccaneers	Carolina League	Pittsburgh Pirates

WASHINGTON

Bellingham	Mariners	Northwest League	Seattle Mariners
Everett	Giants	Northwest League	San Francisco Giants
Spokane	Indians	Northwest League	San Diego Padres
Tacoma	Tigers	Pacific Coast League	Oakland Athletics
Yakima	Bears	Northwest League	Los Angeles Dodgers

WEST VIRGINIA

Bluefield	Orioles	Appalachian League	Baltimore Orioles
Charleston	Wheelers	South Atlantic League	Cincinnati Reds
Huntington	Cubs	Appalachian League	Chicago Cubs
Princeton	Reds	Appalachian League	Cincinnati Reds

WISCONSIN

Appleton	Foxes	Midwest League	Seattle Mariners
Beloit	Brewers	Midwest League	Milwaukee Brewers
Madison	Hatters	Midwest League	St. Louis Cardinals

CANADA

ALBERTA

Calgary	Cannons	Pacific Coast League	Seattle Mariners
Edmonton	Trappers	Pacific Coast League	Florida Marlins
Lethbridge	Mounties	Pioneer League	Independent
Medicine Hat	Blue Jays	Pioneer League	Toronto Blue Jays

BRITISH COLUMBIA

Vancouver	Canadians	Pacific Coast League	California Angels

ONTARIO

Ottawa	Lynx	International League	Montreal Expos
St. Catherines	Blue Jays	New York-Penn League	Toronto Blue Jays
Thunder Bay	Whiskey Jacks	Northern League	Independent
Welland	Pirates	New York-Penn League	Pittsburgh Pirates

MINOR LEAGUE STATS

ALL-TIME LEADERS, INDIVIDUAL SINGLE SEASON

BATTING AVERAGE (200 AT-BATS)

PLAYER	AVG	TEAM	LEAGUE	YEAR
Gary Redus	.462	Billings	Pioneer	1978
Bill Krieg	.452	Rockford	Western Association	1896
Ike Boone	.448	Mission	Pacific Coast	1930
Frank Saucier	.446	Wichita Falls	Big State	1949
Willie Aikens	.443	Puebla/Tidewater	Mexican/International	1986
Angel Aragon	.443	Long Branch	Atlantic	1914
Billy O'Connell	.442	Richmond	Blue Grass	1912
Robert Joe Schmidt	.441	Duluth	Northern	1939
Murray Franklin	.439	Beckley	Mountain State	1938
Humberto Vargas	.438	Vera Cruz/Guanajuato	Mexican/Mex. Center	1966
Jimmie Collins	.438	Chihuahua	Mexican	1979
Francis Bonair	.435	Hornell	PONY	1956
Bill Durster	.434	Salina/Tulsa	Southwestern/Western	1926
Carl East	.433	Anniston	Georgia-Alabama	1926
T. P. Osborne	.432	Mt. Pleasant	East Texas	1924
Russ Snyder	.432	McAlester	Sooner State	1953
Neal Cobb	.432	Crestview	Alabama-Florida	1954
Kelly	.431	Poughkeepsie	Atlantic	1914
Tony Antista	.430	Bisbee	Arizona State	1930

RUNS

PLAYER	RUNS	TEAM	LEAGUE	YEAR
Tony Lazzeri	202	Salt Lake City	Pacific Coast	1925
Gus Suhr	196	San Francisco	Pacific Coast	1929
Lee Najo	195	Okmulgee	Western Association	1925
Ike Boone	195	Missions	Pacific Coast	1929
Frank Demaree	190	Los Angeles	Pacific Coast	1934
Buck Frierson	188	Sherman-Denison	Big State	1947
Joe Bauman	188	Roswell	Longhorn	1954
Sammy Davis	187	Okmulgee	Western Association	1924
Orlando Moreno	186	Big Spring	Longhorn	1947
Bob Crues	185	Amarillo	West Texas–New Mexico	1947

HITS

PLAYER	HITS	TEAM	LEAGUE	YEAR
Paul Strand	325	Salt Lake City	Pacific Coast	1923
Ike Boone	323	Missions	Pacific Coast	1929
Oscar Eckhardt	315	Missions	Pacific Coast	1933
Smead Jolley	314	San Francisco	Pacific Coast	1929
Jay Kirke	282	Louisville	American Association	1921

DOUBLES

PLAYER	2BS	TEAM	LEAGUE	YEAR
Lyman Lamb	100	Tulsa	Western	1924
Paul Waner	75	San Francisco	Pacific Coast	1925
Roy Lashe	73	Salt Lake City	Pacific Coast	1924
Leslie Sheehan	72	Salt Lake City	Pacific Coast	1923
Robert Holland	72	Seattle	Pacific Coast	1930
Ervin Beck	71	Toledo	Interstate	1900
Lyman Lamb	71	Tulsa	Western	1923
Roy Eldred	71	Seattle	Pacific Coast	1923
Roy Eldred	71	Seattle	Pacific Coast	1924
Jack Lelivelt	70	Omaha	Western	1921
Bruno Williams	70	Dallas	Texas	1925
Buzz Arlett	70	Oakland	Pacific Coast	1929

TRIPLES

PLAYER	3BS	TEAM	LEAGUE	YEAR
Jack Cross	32	London	Michigan–Ontario	1925
Walter Shaner	30	Lincoln	Western	1925
Dusty Cooke	30	Asheville	South Atlantic	1928
Eddie Moore	30	Ft. Worth	Texas	1929
Pete Rose	30	Tampa	Florida State	1961
Guy Tutweiller	29	Providence	International	1914
Jo Jo White	29	Ft. Smith	Western	1929
Burt Horton	29	El Paso	Arizona–Texas	1941

HOME RUNS

PLAYER	HRS	TEAM	LEAGUE	YEAR
Joe Bauman	72	Roswell	Longhorn	1954
Joe Hauser	69	Minneapolis	American Association	1933
Bob Crues	69	Amarillo	West Texas–New Mexico	1948
Dick Stuart	66	Lincoln	Western	1956
Bob Lennon	64	Nashville	Southern Association	1954
Joe Hauser	63	Baltimore	International	1930
Moose Clabaugh	62	Tyler	East Texas	1926
Ken Guettler	62	Shreveport	Texas	1956
Tony Lazzeri	60	Salt Lake City	Pacific Coast	1925
Frosty Kennedy	60	Plainview	Southwestern	1956

RUNS BATTED IN

PLAYER	RBIS	TEAM	LEAGUE	YEAR
Bob Crues	254	Amarillo	West Texas–New Mexico	1948
Joe Bauman	224	Roswell	Longhorn	1954
Tony Lazzeri	222	Salt Lake City	Pacific Coast	1925
Ike Boone	218	Mission	Pacific Coast	1929
Buck Frierson	197	Sherman-Denison	Big State League	1947
Glenn Burns	197	Lamesa	West Texas–New Mexico	1951
Clarence Kraft	196	Ft. Worth	Texas	1924
Pud Miller	196	Wichita Falls	Big State	1947
Virg Richardson	196	Lubbock	West Texas–New Mexico	1948
Earl Smith	195	Phoenix	Arizona–Texas	1954

STOLEN BASES

PLAYER	SBS	TEAM	LEAGUE	YEAR
Vince Coleman	145	Macon	South Atlantic	1983
Donell Nixon	144	Bakersfield	California	1983
James Johnston	124	San Francisco	Pacific Coast	1913
Jeff Stone	123	Spartanburg	South Atlantic	1981
Alan Wiggins	120	Lodi	California	1980
Allan Lewis	116	Leesburg	Florida State	1966
Ovid Nicholson	111	Frankfort	Blue Grass	1912
Maynard DeWitt	110	Zanesville	Ohio State	1946
Otis Nixon	108	Columbus (49)	American Association	1982
		Nashville (59)	Southern Association	1982
Lyle Judy	107	Springfield	Western Association	1935

STRIKEOUTS

PLAYER	SOS	TEAM	LEAGUE	YEAR
Bill Kennedy	456	Rocky Mount	Coastal Plain	1946
Virgil Trucks	418	Andalusia	Alabama–Florida	1938
Harry Vickers	409	Seattle	Pacific Coast	1906
Yancey Ayers	390	Richmond	Virginia	1913
Eddie Albrecht	389	Pine Bluff	Cotton States	1949
Vean Gregg	376	Portland	Pacific Coast	1910
Bob Schultz	361	Fulton	Kitty	1946
Larry Jackson	351	Fresno	California	1952
Bob Upton	346	Jacksonville	Gulf Coast	1950
Mike Conovan	345	Jackson	Kitty League	1952

WINS (SINCE 1902)

PLAYER	WINS	TEAM	LEAGUE	YEAR
Doc Newton	39	Los Angeles	Pacific Coast	1904
Harry Vickers	39	Seattle	Pacific Coast	1906
George Boehler	38	Tulsa	Western	1922
Oscar Jones	37	Los Angeles	California	1902
Glenn Liebhardt	35	Memphis	Southern Association	1906
Bugs Raymond	35	Charleston	South Atlantic	1907
Jackie May	35	Vernon	Pacific Coast	1922
Bill Thomas	35	Houma	Evangeline	1946

TEAMS WINNING 20 OR MORE CONSECUTIVE GAMES

YEAR	TEAM	LEAGUE	WINS
1902	Corsicana	Texas	27
1902	Charlotte	North Carolina	25
1903	Jersey City	Eastern	24
1911	Austin	Texas	22
1912	Wilkes-Barre	New York State	25
1920	Baltimore	International	25
1921	Baltimore	International	27
1943	Los Angeles	Pacific Coast	21
1946	Peekskill	North Atlantic	26
1947	Stockton	California	26
1966	Spartanburg	Western Carolinas	25
1966	St. Petersburg	Florida State	22
1986	Johnson City	Appalachian	23
1987	Salt Lake City	Pioneer	29
1990	Elizabethton	Appalachian	20

Reprinted from the *Minor League Encyclopedia*, published by Baseball America, Inc., Durham, N.C.

BIBLIOGRAPHY

Beard, Gordon. *Birds on the Wing: The Story of the Baltimore Orioles.* Garden City, N.Y.: Doubleday & Co., 1967.

Lamb, David. *Stolen Season.* New York: Random House, 1991.

Lange, Fred. *The History of Baseball in California and the Pacific Coast Leagues, 1847–1938.* Oakland, Calif.: self-published, 1938.

Lieb, Frederick. *The Baltimore Orioles.* New York: Putnam, 1955.

Linthurst, Randolph. *The Newark Bears.* Trenton, N.J.: White Eagle Publishing, 1978.

Mayer, Ron. *The 1937 Newark Bears.* New York: Wise & Co., 1982.

National Association of Professional Baseball Leagues, eds. *The Story of Minor League Baseball.* Columbus, Ohio: self-published, 1953.

Obojski, Robert. *Bush League.* New York: Macmillan, 1975.

O'Neal, Bill. *The American Association.* Austin, Tex.: Eakin Press, 1990.

———. *The International League.* Austin, Tex.: Eakin Press, 1988.

———. *The Pacific Coast League.* Austin, Tex.: Eakin Press, 1990.

———. *The Texas League: A Century of Baseball.* Austin, Tex.: Eakin Press, 1989.

Petersen, Robert. *Only the Ball Was White: A History of Legendary Black Players and All-Black Professional Teams.* New York: McGraw-Hill, 1984.

Simpson, Allen, ed. *Baseball America's Directory.* Durham, N.C.: Baseball America, Inc., 1993.

Society for American Baseball Research, eds. *Minor League Baseball Stars, Vols. I, II, III.* Birmingham, Ala.: EBSCO Media, 1992.

Sullivan, Neil. *The Minors.* New York: St. Martin's Press, 1990.

INDEX

(Page numbers in *italic* refer to illustrations.)

National Association, 20, 30–31, 33, *117*

National Baseball Federation, 47

National League, 21, 30, 33, 59, 66, 92, 96, 99; formation of, 19; minor leaguers' games against, 25–26

Native Americans, 44–45, 46

Natural, The, 143

Nebraska State League, 99–100

Necciai, Ron, 140–41

Negro American League, 66

Negro Association League, 66

Negro Leagues, 46, 66–70, *68,* 120; advertisement for, *67;* cultural role of, 70; level of play in, 68; schedules of, 67–68

Negro National League, 66, 67, 81

Newark Star Eagle, 118, *120*

Newark teams, 27, 39, 78, 79; Bears, *50, 53, 69, 75, 86,* 101, 115–16, 118–22, *118–23,* 136; Domestics, 118; Eagles, 120; Peppers, 118

New Britain (Conn.) Red Sox, *17*

New Brunswick and Maine League, 54

New Castle (Pa.) team, 27

New England League, 30, 82–83, 116–17; boxscores for, *78*

New Haven Ravens, 152

Newhouser, Hal, 107

New Orleans teams, 63; Black Eagles, 67

newsletters, *91*

newspapers, 29, 57, 75, *105,* 108, *120;* box scores in, *78; Boys World* supplement in, 70; photographs in, 34, 70–71; schedules printed in, 40; scoreboards of, 40–43, *41*

New York Giants, 25, 27, 45, 56–57, 62–63, 64, 66, 78, 81, 84, *86,* 94, 95, 97, 99, 118, 122, 127

New York–Penn League, 150

New York State League, 29, 30

New York Yankees, 45, 59, 63, 66, 71, 79, 81, 94, 96, 99, 101, 112, 121, 122, 137

nicknames, 14–15

Nicollet Park (Minneapolis, Minn.), *35, 54, 73*

night baseball, 104–7

1929 stock-market crash, 87

Nogales Crows (Sonora, Mexico), 63–64

no-hitters, 37, 81, 140, 141

North Carolina League, 12

North Carolina State League, 12, 107

Northeast Arkansas League, 40

Northern League, 87, *112,* 138, 147, 150, 152–53

Northwestern League, 20, 21, 54

Northwest League, 139, 150

novels about baseball, 34

O

Oakland (Calif.) Stadium, *88*

Oakland (Calif.) teams, 23, *23, 76, 89;* G&M's, 89; Oaks, *88, 96*

Oates, Johnny, 148

O'Connell, Jimmie, 64, 65, 84

O'Connor, Dave, 34

O'Doul, Lefty, 94–95

Ogden, Jack, 62

Oldfield, Barney, 93

old timers games, *31,* 104, 155

Olympic baseball, 144, 148

Ontario League, 87

opening day, *35, 37, 38, 54,* 59, *75, 76, 93, 120*

Orioles Park (Baltimore), 15, 62

O'Rourke, Jim, 81

Ottawa teams, 56; Lynx, *150,* 152

P

Pacific Coast International League, 54

Pacific Coast League (PCL), 43, 57, 63, 71, 77, 80, 82, 88–97, *90, 91,* 100, 108, 116, 127, *135,* 144, 150; ballparks of, *88,* 91–92, *92, 93;* former major leaguers in, 93–96; franchises of, 89–90; Hollywood stars and, 90–91

Pacific Northwest League, 30

Page Fence Giants, 27, 28

Paige, Satchel, 46, 47, 120

Panther Park (Fort Worth, Tex.), 114

Parks, Jim, 37

Parkway Field (Louisville, Ky.), 104, *113,* 114

Pasirba, John, 141

Patkin, Max, *152,* 154

Patterson, Dwight, 64, 81

Pawtucket (R.I.) Red Sox, 150–51

Pendleton, Ike, 34

pennants, *17*

Penn State Association, 107

Pennsylvania Colored Giants, 67, *77*

Pennsylvania State League, 21

Petersburg (Va.) team, 37

Pfeffer, Fred, 25

Phelin, Marty, *123*

Philadelphia teams: A's, 84, 62, 66, 140; Athletics, 99; Phillies, 66, 94, 141; Stars, 67

Phillips, Handy Andy, 139

Piedmont League, 12, 103

Pierce, Billy, *136*

Pierce, Paul, 149

Pierce, Robert, 47

Pilette, Edward "Old Folks," 80

Pilot Field (Buffalo, N.Y.), *149*

Pioneer League, 107, 150

Pitts, Edwin "Alabama," *106,* 110–12

Pittsburgh teams, 19; Pirates, 30, 33, 114, 141

player-managers, 83, 140

Players' League, 20, 57

playoff system, 107

Poffo, Randall (Randy "Macho Man" Savage), 139

Point Isabel (Tex.) Tarpons, *36*

Polo Grounds (New York City), 34

Ponce de Leon Hotel (Saint Augustine, Fla.), 51

Pony League, 56, 107

Portland (Maine) Pilots, *130*

Poughkeepsie (N.Y.) team, 130

Powell, Abner, 29

Powell, Boog, 140

Powell, William, 91

Pride, Charley, 140

Prince William County (Va.) Cannons, 152

prison teams, *106,* 110–11

programs, *90, 130, 134, 135, 142, 146, 151*

promotions, 104, 154; beauty contests, *131;* knothole gangs, 74, 104, *131,* 155; Ladies' Day, 29, *74,* 104, 130; old timers games, *31,* 104, 155

Provincial League, 54

Puget Sound League, 21

Pulaski (Va.) team, 140

Q

Quebec-Ontario-Vermont League, 54

Quebec Provincial League, 54

Quincy (Ill.) team, 103

R

racism, 27–28, 141

Radcliffe, Double Duty, 80

radio, 125

rain checks, 29

rained-out games, 22–23, 43

Rain or Shine, 83

PHOTOGRAPHY CREDITS

Photographers and collectors who have contributed photography to this book are:

AP/Worldwide Photos: p. 156 (M. Jordan)

Courtesy of Arizona Historical Society, Tucson: pp. 61, 62, 65, 127

Austin Archives Division, Texas State Library: p. 36

Austin History Center, Austin Public Library, TX: pp. 18, 128–29, 132, 133

Babe Ruth Museum, Baltimore, MD: pp. 10, 11, 58 top and bottom

Baseball America, Durham, NC: pp. 12, 145 top, center, and bottom

Berns County Historical Association, PA, pp. 32, 110

George Beshuzko ©: pp. 4, 8, 16 top and bottom, 17, 142, 146, 150 center, 151 top right

Buffalo Bisons, NY: p. 149

California State Library, Sacramento: pp. 21, 25, 38, 76

Courtesy of the Camden County Historical Society, Camden, NJ: p. 20

Bruce Chadwick Collection: pp. 15, 28, 40, 44, 48, 66, 68, 70, 77, 105, 130, 140

Rory Chadwick ©: pp. 91 bottom left and center, 96, 97 top and bottom, 154, 155

Donald Cohen, pp. 105 right, 160 bottom and top

Dallas Public Library, TX: pp. 124, 131

Durham Bulls (Simon Griffiths), NC: p. 109

Buddy Hassett: p. 101 right, 102

Irvington Historical Collection, Irvington Public Library, NJ: p. 31

Kansas State Historical Society: p. 22

Robert Lowell: p. 117

Midland Angels Baseball Club, TX: pp. 148, 153

Minnesota Historical Society: pp. 6, 54/endpapers, 72, 73 top and bottom

Mutual Welfare League, Ossining Historical Society, NY, p. 106 Linda Naprstek ©: pp. 1, 12 bottom, 24, 26, 39, 67, 71, 90 top, center, and bottom, 91 top and center right, 111 bottom, 134–135, 139, 150 top and bottom, 151 all except top right

National Baseball Library and Archive, Cooperstown, NY: p. 100 top

Oakland Public Library, CA: pp. 23, 88 top and bottom, 89, 92, 93

Joseph M. Overfield: pp. 79 top and bottom right, 108 bottom, 136, 137

Max Patkin: p. 152

Putnam Museum of History and Natural Science, Davenport, Iowa: pp. 42, 98

Harry L. Sears Collection: pp. 13, 14, 35, 43, 46, 49, 50–51, 52, 53, 68 bottom, 69, 70 left, 74 top and bottom, 78 top and bottom, 79 left, 80, 82, 83, 85, 86, 100 bottom, 101 left, 103, 105 top left, 118, 119, 120, 121, 122, 123

Dana Sprague: pp. 55, 87, 112 top and bottom, 114, 126

Tacoma Public Library, WA: pp. 2–3, 41 top, 94, 95, 108 top University of Louisville, Photographic Archives, KY: pp. 37 top and bottom, 41 bottom, 74, 104, 111, 113, 131 top

FOR MARGIE AND RORY

EDITOR: Stephen Brewer

DESIGNER: Patricia Fabricant

PRODUCTION EDITOR: Owen Dugan

PRODUCTION DIRECTOR: Simone René

COPY EDITOR: Amy Hughes

PHOTOGRAPHERS: George Bezushko, Rory Chadwick, Linda Naprstek

Library of Congress Cataloging-in-Publication Data

Chadwick, Bruce.
    Baseball's hometown teams : the story of the minor leagues /
Bruce Chadwick.
        p. cm.
    Includes bibliographical references and index.
    ISBN 1-55859-701-8
    1. Minor league baseball—United States—History.   I. Title.
GV863.A1C426   1994
796.357'64'0973—dc20   94-9253

Text copyright © 1994 Bruce Chadwick. Photography copyright © 1994 George Bezushko, Rory Chadwick, Linda Naprstek. Compilation, including selection, order, and placement of text and images, copyright © 1994 Abbeville Press. All rights reserved under international copyright conventions. No part of this book may be reproduced or utilized in any form or by any means, electronic or mechanical, including photocopying, recording, or by any information storage and retrieval system, without written permission from the publisher. Inquiries should be addressed to Abbeville Publishing Group, 488 Madison Avenue, New York, NY 10022.

Printed and bound in Singapore.

First edition.

ENDPAPERS:
OLD NICOLLET PARK IN MINNEAPOLIS.

PAGE 1:
THE MIDDLE ATLANTIC LEAGUE'S TWENTY-FIFTH
ANNIVERSARY YEARBOOK.

PAGES 2–3:
THE CUSTOMIZED DOUBLE-DECKER BUS THE 1938
TACOMA TIGERS TOOK TO THEIR AWAY GAMES.

PAGE 4:
THE READING PHILLIES HAVE ONE OF THE RICHEST
HISTORIES IN MINOR-LEAGUE BALL.

PAGE 6:
A SINGLE-TIER GRANDSTAND WITH A WOODEN ROOF—
A TYPICAL 1920S BALLPARK.